# BEST PRACTICES FOR OPERATIONAL EXCELLENCE

---

## SIMPLE PROCEDURES THAT WORK FOR MANUFACTURING AND LOGISTICS

LUCA DELLANNA

**Luca Dellanna**

@DellAnnaLuca
Luca-dellanna.com

Fourth edition
September 2025

# ADVANCE PRAISE

"I'm a huge fan of High Output Management and Setting the Table [...] Luca's Best Practices for Operational Excellence took my management to the next level.

**It's been almost a month since I started implementing the principles, but I can already say that I've noticed a significant improvement in my company's morale [...] That feels amazing."**

*— MOLSON HART, VIAHART CEO*

"A worthy read to anyone who feels their business or team is a little out of whack."

*— TAYLOR PEARSON, MUTINY FUND PRINCIPAL*

# INTRODUCTION

I've been working in Operational Excellence for over twelve years, and while that might not sound like much, I've seen hundreds of companies and consulted for dozens. I've witnessed problems and solutions, and I know what works and what doesn't. This book is a practical guide to help you become a more effective manager and solve most workplace challenges. Achieving Operational Excellence is not complicated. It requires some focused effort, but benefits appear quickly if you know where to focus.

The first part describes the Four Principles of Operational Excellence, showing which actions matter and which don't, and highlighting a few high-impact actions you can start implementing today.

The second part presents eight Best Practices: quick tools you can use today to change how your team operates and provide evidence that change is possible: unmotivated employees can become motivated, unproductive ones productive, and previously unreachable objectives achievable.

The third and final part offers a roadmap to extend these changes beyond your team to your plant, office, or organization.

But first, let me begin with a story of change.

———

At the crossroads of the 18th and 19th centuries, a French chemist named Éleuthère Irénée du Pont had to leave the country in a hurry. He had studied under the renowned chemist Lavoisier, but political controversies following the French Revolution forced him to flee. He took a boat to the New Continent to escape jail and, perhaps, the guillotine.

On January 1, 1800, he landed in Delaware. With his chemical expertise, he began operating a gunpowder factory on the Brandywine River. As he soon learned, gunpowder factories exploded frequently. Faced with increasing incidents, injuries, and deaths, he knew something had to change. How he solved the problem would shape the future of Operational Excellence.

Éleuthère du Pont took two initiatives.[1] First, he required the Director (himself) to live inside the factory with his family, putting his own life on the line. Second, he mandated that every new machine be operated for the first time by top management. If it exploded, the manager faced the consequences personally.

Unsurprisingly, the plant's safety improved almost overnight. **Leadership shown through visible, costly actions is powerful.** The gunpowder company gradually grew into one of the world's largest industrial conglomerates, DuPont. Two centuries later, its destiny would eventually cross mine.

Even though I graduated as an automotive engineer, I never worked as one. On a hot summer day, while writing my final thesis, I received a call from the person who would become my first boss. He asked me to join his consulting team in Frankfurt, Germany. Excited and knowing not a word of German, I accepted. I became an employee of DuPont.[2]

While there, I learned a great deal. At the time, the company was considered the world's leading expert in Workplace Safety consulting. I had the chance to work with some of the top experts on the planet, visiting tens of client companies, learning from hundreds of managers and thousands of workers. I listened to their words, their problems, and their aspirations. I observed best practices, analyzed failures, proposed solutions, and followed their implementation. I internalized Operational Excellence.

A few years later, I left to start my own consulting practice. I spent months learning as much as I could about Operational Excellence and speaking with former experts and new clients. Then I developed a framework to help managers improve their company's operational culture.

I now run my consulting practice, helping managers worldwide develop their employees and run operations to their full potential. Yet helping managers one by one limits my leverage. To reach more people, I decided to write this book.

## OUTLINE

This book is divided into three parts.

**The first part covers the Four Principles of Operational Excellence,** which you can leverage to create an Operational Culture worth working in.

**The second part details the Eight Best Practices that turn these principles into visible actions.** I provide step-by-step lists and practical examples to make execution easier.

**The third part offers a roadmap for planning a plant-wide or company-wide change initiative,** securing Top Management buy-in, rolling it out effectively, and ensuring long-term sustainability.

But first, let's explore the importance of Operational Excellence and the costs of a mediocre Operational Culture.

## THE BENEFITS OF OPERATIONAL EXCELLENCE

It is deeply satisfying to see an organization that has achieved Operational Excellence. Managers are focused on tasks where they have the most leverage, no longer running around fixing emergencies. Workers take pride in their work, own their roles, and trust their managers. The workplace is safe, organized, and everyone knows what the company is doing and cares about it.

Unfortunately, few companies practice Operational Excellence. Few managers know how to achieve it, and even fewer prioritize it. While they recognize the benefits, many are not convinced that those benefits are worth the effort.

There are many self-interested reasons to implement Operational Excellence. **Managers of a team with a culture of Operational Excellence are less stressed** (they do not spend their days running after emergencies), **work fewer hours** (when you are effective, you don't have to work overtime), **are more fulfilled** (they become respected by both their subordinates and their boss), **are more valuable** (they and their team become able to hit milestones consistently), **are more employable** (being able to manage a team effectively is a rare and valuable skill), **and are wealthier** (as their team hits their bottom-line results, more money becomes available to be distributed in the form of bonuses).

## OPERATIONAL EXCELLENCE AND MANAGEMENT

The first part of this book, *The Four Principles of Operational Excellence*, focuses on management. The Eight Best Practices, which give the book its title, appear in the second part. This order is intentional: no best practice will be followed by employees if managers cannot set clear objectives and hold people accountable in a fair, transparent, and predictable way.

I urge you to pay close attention to the first part, even if you think you already know management. The concepts here are not the usual boilerplate, and failing to internalize them is the real bottleneck to Operational Excellence. Seeking another best practice without a solid foundation in performance management brings only short-lived satisfaction. True, lasting change in your professional life comes from mastering the Four Principles.

## A MAP

A city map does not show every building or tree. Omitting some details is not a flaw but a feature: it allows the reader to focus on the information that matters and take effective action.

Similarly, this book does not attempt to cover everything about Operational Excellence—it would take a hundred books to do that. Instead, it presents most of what you need to know to take effective action and improve your team's operational culture.

## ANY QUESTIONS?

If you have questions not covered in this book, you can email me at **Luca@Luca-dellanna.com**. I read all messages personally and usually reply within 48 hours.


## TERMINOLOGY

In this book, the following definitions apply: *"Worker"* refers to any employee without subordinates; *"Supervisor"* refers to any employee managing workers; *"Manager"* refers to any employee managing subordinates of any kind (workers, supervisors, or other managers); and *"Top Management"* refers to the CEO and other senior executives, such as C-suite members and Vice Presidents.

Unless otherwise specified, *"your subordinates"* refers to your direct reports only, not their reports.


## DISCLAIMER

*The contents of this book reflect the author's personal experience. While he believes it can help most readers, its advice is highly contextual. Only you know what's best for you. Always use your judgment and consult experts when appropriate. Nothing in this book should be considered medical, financial, investment, or other professional advice. The author is not liable for any consequences arising from the use or misuse of its contents.*

## THE COSTS OF LACKING OPERATIONAL EXCELLENCE

Achieving and maintaining a great Operational Culture requires time and money. However, these investments are small compared to the costs of a mediocre Operational Culture, plagued by structural problems, demotivated employees, and a lack of clarity and trust.

For managers like you, the costs of a mediocre Operational Culture include:

- **Overtime:** Action is slow, and problems aren't addressed unless the manager intervenes. Conversely, in teams with a strong Operational Culture, micromanagement isn't needed, and managers are more likely to leave work on time.

- **Lower bonuses:** Teams with mediocre culture fail to achieve goals or impact the bottom line. Conversely, teams with a great culture contribute effectively, enabling larger bonuses or raises.

- **More stress:** Daily problems create a stressful environment. Conversely, teams with great culture solve problems effectively, creating a low-stress workplace.

- **Less energy:** Managers spend their days "putting out fires." Conversely, in strong cultures, team members solve problems themselves, freeing managers to focus on a few important tasks.

- **Less trust:** In mediocre cultures, career advancement may reward servility or toxic behavior, making trust scarce. Conversely, in strong cultures, people are rewarded for acting in line with Core Values and objectives, creating a trustworthy environment.

- **Less satisfaction:** Overall, mediocre cultures are draining and financially unrewarding, whereas strong Operational Cultures are fulfilling both financially and mentally.

A mediocre Operational Culture is not only harmful to managers but also costly for companies. Some direct costs of lacking Operational Excellence include:

- **Defects:** scrap, rework, customer support, and recalls.

- **Poor logistics:** transportation, storage, and capital immobilization that add no value to the customer.

- **Injuries:** production stoppages and worker benefits.

- **Environmental problems:** fines and legal liabilities.

- **Unethical workplaces:** fines, rogue employees, and the loss of key personnel due to ethical violations.

Indirect costs, however, are even greater:

- **Defects:** damage to brand reputation, impairing customer acquisition and retention.

- **Poor logistics:** production stoppages, unhappy customers, and lost business to competitors.

- **Injuries:** lower quality, reduced morale, and higher insurance costs.

- **Environmental problems:** brand damage and risk of losing operating permits.

- **Unethical workplaces:** brand damage, difficulty attracting and retaining talent, and the need to overpay employees.

- **Poor management:** lower morale and motivation, general underperformance, and the departure of key employees.

In summary, **companies with poor Operational Culture lose their best employees (to injuries, burnout, or competitors) and are left with low-talent or unethical staff, further weakening their culture and creating a difficult-to-break vicious cycle.** For all these reasons, it benefits both managers and companies to pursue Operational Excellence. Let's see how.

# PART I

# THE FOUR PRINCIPLES OF OPERATIONAL EXCELLENCE

**1**

---

# THE 1ST PRINCIPLE OF OPERATIONAL EXCELLENCE

## GOOD MANAGERS SET UNAMBIGUOUS, INDIVIDUAL AND REWARDABLE OBJECTIVES

The most important managerial task is performance management: setting objectives for subordinates and holding them accountable for results. It affects both short-term performance (directing and motivating on current tasks) and long-term performance (communicating values and standards through rewards and consequences).

**Neglecting performance management undermines good results in other areas,** such as communication, hiring, and decision-making. Even skilled managers who fail to show that outcomes follow performance often end up with underperforming teams, despite doing everything else correctly.

Many managers struggle to hold subordinates accountable consistently and constructively. Some hesitate to point out underperformance, fearing it may be excusable. Others fail to reward good performance due to a lack of time or budget. Some are inconsistent or unfair, using unclear criteria or non-performance factors in evaluations. **The common cause of these problems is a failure to set clear objectives. This is the root of most performance management challenges.**

## THE TWO PROBLEMS OF SETTING AMBIGUOUS OBJECTIVES

Managers who set ambiguous objectives face two problems. First, performance suffers. **The more ambiguous an objective, the higher the chance a worker misinterprets it or avoids tasks they are uncomfortable with, ultimately affecting the result.**

Second, **ambiguity makes it harder to hold subordinates accountable.** Employees can argue they fulfilled the request, making it difficult for managers to deliver consequences like feedback, reprimands, or disciplinary actions. Even when managers follow through, subordinates may feel unfairly judged, leading to frustration and lost motivation.

In short, **managers who set unclear objectives tend to have underperforming subordinates and struggle to hold them accountable.**

## A QUICK TEST

Here are three questions to help you assess whether you are clear enough while setting objectives:

- **Do your subordinates spring into action, or do they dwell in confusion?** Clear objectives are actionable, while unclear ones drain confidence and momentum.

- **If a subordinate fails to meet an objective, do you feel comfortable holding them accountable, and do they feel it's fair?** Awkwardness or defensiveness signals insufficient clarity.

- **Do you and your subordinates always agree on their performance?** Disagreements indicate unclear standards.

## THE 3 ATTRIBUTES OF GOOD OBJECTIVES

Good managers set objectives with three attributes: unambiguous, individual, and rewardable. Let's see them one by one.

1. **Good objectives are UNAMBIGUOUS.** Managers make objectives clear by painting a visual description of what success looks like, then asking subordinates to restate their understanding in their own words. This ensures employees cannot misunderstand the objective and managers cannot claim they were unclear, allowing proper accountability.

2. **Good objectives are INDIVIDUAL.** Managers focus objectives on what subordinates can impact through their own contributions. This prevents employees from excusing underperformance by blaming team shortcomings.

3. **Good objectives are REWARDABLE.** Managers set objectives that are ambitious yet achievable. If objectives are too modest, subordinates may meet them but fail to generate enough value to justify rewards, leading to frustration or disengagement. Ambitious objectives ensure that, upon success, the company generates sufficient benefit to reward the employee appropriately.

Objectives must also be realistic. If they feel unattainable, most subordinates will act as if the potential reward doesn't exist, while a few may overwork themselves to the point of burnout.

Most managers understand the importance of these principles but fail to apply them consistently for the six reasons summarized in the following table *(next page)*.

| Objective is... | Cause | Explanation |
|---|---|---|
| Ambiguous | The manager is incompetent. | The manager does not know how to set clear objectives or why it is important to do so. |
| Ambiguous | The manager wants to retain political power. | The blurrier the objectives, the more subjective the manager can be in their rewarding and thus gain power from their ability to apply such subjectivity. |
| Ambiguous | The manager is afraid they won't be able to follow-up with rewards or punishments. | The blurrier the objectives, the easier it is for the manager to confabulate a reason why consequences should not follow results or lack thereof. |
| Ambiguous | The manager is afraid their team will not be able to produce satisfying results anyway. | The blurrier the objectives, the easier it is for the manager to justify to his boss why his team underperformed, but neither he nor individual members should be held accountable. |
| Collective | The manager dreads having difficult conversation with individual subordinates. | The manager assigns responsibilities to groups only so that individual responsibility is unclear and cannot be rewarded or punished. This does not mean that good managers do not use group objectives, but doing so is not sufficient; it is also necessary to use individual ones. |
| Unrewardable | The manager does not respect their capacities or their subordinates' and ends up assigning too conservative objectives. | Objectives should not be set so that they are comfortable but so that good things happen if they are achieved. |

In all but one row of the table, **managers fail to set clear objectives, not due to a lack of skill, but because they believe unclear objectives are the optimal choice.**

## THE VICIOUS CIRCLE OF LOOSE PERFORMANCE MANAGEMENT

One notable example of this phenomenon is the vicious circle of loose performance management. Failing to consistently link individual outcomes to performance worsens the underperformance problems. **Once a manager lets someone off the hook, it sets a precedent, making it easier for others to argue for leniency.** This makes future consistency even harder and further erodes the team's Operational Culture.

**Good managers recognize this cycle and prevent it by setting clear objectives and applying consequences consistently.** As a result, their workers understand what is expected of them, and managers can confidently carry out performance management.

In short, **bad managers describe objectives that can be understood. Good managers describe objectives that cannot be misinterpreted.**

## THRIVING IN A DYSFUNCTIONAL CULTURE

Often, managers find themselves in a dysfunctional culture lacking clarity and consistency. Many respond by adopting the same behaviors: setting unclear objectives and letting underperformance go unpunished. Their reaction to a lack of clarity and consistency is to behave with a similar lack of clarity and consistency.

However, by trying to fit in, they dig a deeper hole for themselves. **Because they set unclear and unambitious objectives, they cannot reward those employees who performed and cannot punish those who didn't.**

As a result, the team underperforms, the manager loses confidence in themselves and the team, and next time they set even more ambiguous, collective, and unrewardable goals. This is a vicious cycle that occurs whenever managers act reactively.

Good managers, in contrast, are proactive. Even in a culture lacking clarity and consistency, they set unambiguous, individual, and rewardable objectives. They know this makes performance management easier and helps break the vicious cycle.

**Good managers do not wait for the perfect environment to do their work; instead, they realize that it is *their* job to create a conducive environment.**

## GUILT AND SHAME

Guilt and shame in a manager are signs of insufficient clarity, individuality, or ambition in delegation. The more a subordinate could mistakenly believe they did a good job when they didn't, the more uncomfortable a manager feels holding them accountable. None of this would have occurred if the objectives had been unmistakably clear.

**Good managers recognize guilt or shame as a signal that they haven't set clear, individual, and rewardable objectives.**

They use these feelings as a cue to have an individual discussion with their subordinates, acknowledge the lack of clarity, and set new objectives with the three key attributes.

Bad managers react to guilt and shame with avoidance; good ones use them as a sign that they should bring more clarity when setting objectives.

In the absence of shame, management is an incredibly simple job. Clarity is what prevents shame from becoming part of the equation.

## LACK OF MOTIVATION

When good managers notice a lack of motivation in their subordinates, they see it as a signal of unclear expectations. This lack of clarity can take three forms:

- **A lack of clarity of objectives:** Unclear objectives leave subordinates unsure of what to do next. This undecidedness is often mistaken for a lack of motivation.

- **A lack of clarity of personal impact:** When objectives are not individual, subordinates are uncertain about the scope and importance of their contribution. They may wait for others to act or avoid taking initiative, resulting in less proactive effort.

- **A lack of clarity of individual outcomes:** When objectives aren't tied to clear, performance-dependent outcomes, subordinates are less motivated to act beyond their comfort zone.

## GOOD PERFORMANCE MANAGEMENT IS EMPOWERING

Managers who are relentless in applying the appropriate consequences to the performance of their subordinates are not selfish. On the contrary, great managers understand that doing so benefits their subordinates. In companies lacking consistent performance management, workers underperform. As a result, managers may be unable to secure the budget for bonuses, raises, or promotions, and in the worst case, may have to lay off team members. Neither outcome benefits the employees.

Great managers also know that performance management helps subordinates realize their potential. Often, employees must step out of their comfort zone to meet objectives and require external incentives to do so. Managers provide these through trustworthy promises of positive outcomes for success and negative ones for failure.

Every employee benefits from reaching their potential, gaining satisfaction, self-respect, salary, and job security. Clear, ambitious objectives and fair consequences are therefore helpful and generous. Managers who are ambiguous and inconsistent, by contrast, are selfish, prioritizing their comfort over their subordinates' development.

## GOOD PERFORMANCE MANAGEMENT IS HUMAN

Some managers are extremely consistent in performance management but set excessively ambitious objectives. While this may boost productivity in the short term, it inevitably leads to long-term burnout. Some employees may feel objectives are unreachable or not worth the effort, while others overwork themselves to the point of breakdown. The result is the same: a team drained of energy.

Great managers know objectives must be ambitious yet human. Occasionally, they may require a performance burst, such as meeting a rush order from a top customer. But even then, they ensure two things: first, that the extra effort is properly rewarded (celebration, time off, bonuses, or development opportunities); second, that it does not become the norm. **Temporary workload spikes are healthy, whereas chronic overtime signals structural problems.**

(Similarly, **chronic overtime is a sign of a dysfunctional manager who tries to cover their effectiveness problem by throwing more time and energy at problems.**)

Great managers work with their subordinates for long-term sustainability. They manage their own and their team's energy, ensure that work and consequences are sustainable, and act in good faith. They are also firm with those unwilling to adopt the same long-term collaboration principles, ensuring either alignment or parting ways to save everyone's time.

## GOOD PERFORMANCE MANAGEMENT MEETS EMPLOYEES WHERE THEY ARE WITHOUT LOWERING LONG-TERM EXPECTATIONS

Managers often face one or more underperforming subordinates. In such cases, immediately setting ambitious goals is ineffective, as underperforming employees may see them as unattainable and respond with indifference.

**Indifference and laziness usually stem from forgetting that good outcomes follow good performance.** This "amnesia" has two main causes: previous managers failing to reward good performance or punish poor performance, and a loss of confidence in one's ability to succeed.

**When dealing with an indifferent subordinate, managers must teach both that good performance is achievable and that it leads to positive individual outcomes.** Focusing only on results while ignoring the subordinate's belief in their capability leads to frustration. (That said, if the bottleneck is skill, the manager must focus on developing the required know-how.)

The proper approach is to set small, attainable objectives and acknowledge improvements consistently, through praise or even a simple thank you. Over a few weeks, progress will follow. Once the subordinate sees that good performance is achievable and rewarded, gradually raise expectations, eventually leading to sustainable high performance and motivation.

The key is to recognize and praise small improvements while never tolerating stagnation or setbacks. Meet subordinates where they are, but maintain the expectation that within a few months, they should be on par with the rest of the team.

(Of course, if they repeatedly fail to meet even small, attainable objectives, it may be necessary to part ways.)

## OBJECTIVES AND ALIGNMENT

**Bad managers rely on communication to achieve alignment. Conversely, good managers achieve it by rewarding behaviors that support the organization's objectives and addressing those that don't.**

## MANAGEMENT DEBT

Whenever managers take the "easy choice" by sacrificing clarity, fairness, or consistency to avoid a difficult conversation or decision, they incur **management debt**: a short-term gain that must eventually be repaid with interest.

Management debt arises because employees react negatively to unclear, unfair, or inconsistent management. As the consequences of tough versus easy choices seem uncertain, employees themselves start making "easy choices," compromising performance, quality, and teamwork.

The more managers repeatedly take easy choices, the more subordinates follow suit.

The term **management debt** was coined by A16Z cofounder Ben Horowitz. In *The Hard Thing About Hard Things*, he identifies three sources: placing two people in the same position on the org chart, overcompensating a key employee to match an external offer, and lacking a performance management or feedback process. These correspond, respectively, to a lack of clarity, fairness, and consistency, as detailed in the following table *(next page)*.

| Source of management debt | Corresponds to... | Explanation |
|---|---|---|
| Putting two in the box | Lack of clarity | Assigning two people to the same position causes a lack of clarity about who is responsible for what and about whose orders and priorities are to be followed |
| Overcompensating an employee who received another job offer | Lack of fairness | Undercompensating an employee until he is offered another job and then overcompensating him is doubly unfair: to the employee himself before he is offered the job and to the rest of his team afterwards. |
| No performance management / employee feedback process | Lack of consistency | Once clear objectives have been issued, performance management is mostly about consistency in applying consequences. |

Good managers minimize management debt by consistently setting unambiguous, individual, and rewardable objectives and holding their subordinates accountable for them. This approach prevents far more costly and difficult problems down the line.

After all, it is easier to spend a career making hard choices than paying for the consequences of easy ones.

## SUMMARY

**Bad managers fail to set clear objectives due to mental patterns that make them believe unclear objectives are better. In doing so, they remove employees' motivation to achieve their goals and make it uncomfortable to follow up on individual outcomes tied to performance.**

Good managers, in contrast, devote time and energy to setting objectives that are unambiguous, individual, and rewardable. Failing to do so is failing their subordinates, who rely on clear guidance toward meaningful objectives that, when achieved, produce positive outcomes for both the organization and the individuals who contributed.

**2**

———

# THE 2ND PRINCIPLE OF OPERATIONAL EXCELLENCE

## GOOD MANAGERS DE-RISK DELEGATION

Many managers are so afraid of being perceived as micromanagers that they adopt an excessively hands-off approach during delegation.

However, **the opposite of micromanagement isn't good management but a lack of management.**

Good managers are both thorough enough during their delegation process to set their delegees up for success without making them feel like they're micromanaged.

This chapter explains how they do that.

## SPECIFICITY INCREASES FREEDOM

Some managers believe that the less they describe a delegated task, the more freedom the delegee feels.

In reality, **vague objectives don't create freedom but paralysis.** Instead of springing into action on a well-defined task, the delegee sits in doubt and confusion, wondering about their exact responsibilities, available resources, expected time, and any sub-objectives or boundaries their manager has in mind. Answering these questions takes time and slows action. Unless they ask directly, delegees can never be sure what's in their manager's mind, which erodes their confidence. The mental toll makes them slower and less effective.

This isn't always true. A small percentage of employees are so smart and proactive that they can execute even the least-defined task. But these are rare, and unless you work with an extraordinary team, you should assume yours needs direction.

## GOOD SPECIFICITY AND BAD SPECIFICITY

Of course, just as it's possible to be too vague, it's also possible to be too specific. The key is whether you're specific about what matters or what doesn't.

**Being specific on what matters is good:** be clear about what success looks like, what resources (budget, people, time) the delegee can use, what boundaries they must respect, and any procedures critical for you to consider the task a success.

Conversely, **being specific about what doesn't matter is bad:** prescribing aesthetic details or non-mandatory procedures based on personal preferences is usually a bad idea.

The line between the two is blurry, which is why management is more art than science. Hopefully, the rest of the chapter will help you decide what to mention when delegating and what to leave out.

## WHAT YOUR DELEGEE NEEDS TO KNOW

**What success looks like.** If you use metrics, pair the numbers with a vivid description. For example: "Increase supermarket penetration to 30%; I want people to see our products not just at specialized distributors but also during their weekly shopping." Visual descriptions may seem redundant, but they add clarity and engagement.

**What resources they can leverage.** Specify the budget, tools, and colleagues available. You've assigned your delegee's precious time to this task because it's important; don't let them underinvest.

**What's enough, too little, or too much.** Both under-delivery and over-delivery are undesirable.[1] Be explicit about what counts as enough, too little, and too much.

**Must-follow procedures or boundaries.** Sometimes a specific procedure is mandatory due to policy or regulation; other times, multiple approaches work. Be clear about how much freedom of choice they have.

**Most likely failure modes.** Imagine your delegee works hard but still fails. What are the most likely reasons? Pointing them out dramatically improves their chances of success.

**Anything else that truly matters.** Keep personal preferences to a minimum, but if something is important to you, say it. It's better to add one extra specification than to be unable to praise a delegee who met all stated requirements but missed an unstated preference. Few things are more demotivating than working hard and not hearing "Great job!" from your boss.

This last point is crucial. To keep your team engaged, they should succeed at least 70% of the time and receive praise for it. At the same time, you don't want to praise work that isn't genuinely great. That's why it's essential to take the time to set them up for success from the start.

## TAKE THE TIME TO DELEGATE PROPERLY

Many managers delegate too briefly because they feel short on time. Yet they're short on time precisely because they spend much of their week fixing the consequences of unclear delegation.

Great managers know that every extra minute spent setting delegees up for success saves at least two minutes of problem-solving later.

## NEVER DELEGATE NON-TRIVIAL TASKS OVER EMAIL

When delegating a task over email, delegees are far less likely to ask clarifying questions. In contrast, when delegating in person or on a phone or video call, it's much easier for them to ask, and for you to gauge their understanding. You can read tone of voice and facial expressions to see whether they feel confident or doubtful. For example, if you notice a frown, it's a sign you haven't been clear enough and should clarify.

## DERISK, DERISK, DERISK

> "Because some of the hardest accountability problems for a manager to navigate crop up when your team can't get their work done because they're dependent on the work of one or more other teams, it's important to de-risk those dependencies."
>
> — *CLAIRE HUGHES JOHNSON*

You shouldn't do your subordinate's work for them, but taking a few extra minutes during delegation to de-risk the task together not only increases their chances of success but also creates a fair basis for accountability.

If problems arise, you can hold them responsible for what is truly within their control, while avoiding unfairly blaming them for external factors or circumstances. At the same time, it reduces the discomfort managers often feel when they partially see themselves as responsible for a subordinate's failure, making the process fairer and clearer for both parties.

## SUPERCLARITY

Most managers should communicate more clearly. Their usual standard is "clear enough to be understood," but that's not enough. If you're only clear enough to be understandable, instead of being so clear that you cannot be misunderstood, your subordinates may misinterpret you. If the misunderstanding isn't quickly corrected, it leads to blame and resentment. That's why **you must be superclear: not just clear enough so that you can be understood, but clear enough so that you cannot be misunderstood.**

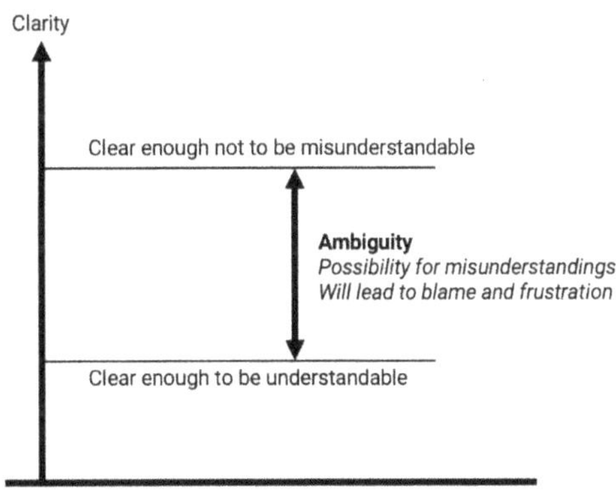

## WHY AREN'T MANAGERS SUPERCLEAR?

Often, this is a deliberate choice. Some managers fear that being super-clear might insult their interlocutor's intelligence. While that may be true, vagueness erodes trust and respect far more.

Others avoid clarity to leave room for creativity, yet it's possible to be crystal clear about the objective while allowing freedom in how to achieve it. By contrast, unclear goals can cause paralysis or excessive caution.

Finally, some managers aren't clear because they themselves don't yet know what they want. That's why it's wise to take a few seconds to clarify the task in your own mind before starting a delegation.

## HOW TO BECOME SUPERCLEAR

The theory is simple: be so clear you cannot be misunderstood – and, to avoid micromanaging, focus on the outcome you need, not on how to achieve it. The practice is harder. Three actions help:

- **Be concrete and give examples.** Don't just cite abstract concepts like "be ethical." Describe actions: what does an ethical person do? And an unethical one?

- **Pre-empt misunderstandings.** Ask yourself, "If my interlocutor walks away with a different understanding, what might they have missed?" Then proactively add information to close the gap.

- **Ask them to rephrase their understanding of the task.** This catches omissions and misunderstandings. Prestigious professions such as surgeons and pilots do this routinely.

Of these three tips, the third meets the most resistance, as managers fear it may seem distrustful. In this case, shift the burden to yourself by saying, "I might have forgotten something important; can you repeat your understanding of the task so I can check?"

## THE IMPORTANCE OF SETTING YOUR DELEGEES UP FOR SUCCESS

Let me conclude this chapter as I began it, addressing the common fear of being seen as a micromanager.

As a manager, you should balance two needs: (1) do not do your subordinates' work, and (2) set them up for success. The latter is crucial because a subordinate who isn't successful will not only underperform but also quickly lose motivation and trust in you. They may begin to believe it's not worth putting effort into the tasks you delegate, since nothing good will come of them anyway.

This is why, when delegating, you should take the time to derisk their tasks and provide the context and tools they need to succeed.

As a rule of thumb, if your delegees do not satisfactorily complete about 70–80% of your assigned tasks, or if you spend more time fixing their mistakes than delegating, it means you are not investing enough time upfront to set them up for success.

## CHAPTER SUMMARY

When delegating a task, take the time to set your delegees up for success. Be explicit about what success looks like, the resources they can use, what constitutes enough, too little, or too much, any must-follow procedures or boundaries, likely failure modes, and anything else that truly matters.

Spend a few minutes preparing by asking yourself how you might be misunderstood, then proactively prevent that misunderstanding.

Do not let the fear of being seen as a micromanager stop you from doing your job: setting your people up for success.

**3**

---

# THE 3RD PRINCIPLE OF OPERATIONAL EXCELLENCE

## GOOD MANAGERS DEMONSTRATE PRIORITIES WITH VISIBLE COSTLY ACTIONS

Most companies genuinely want their Core Values, such as sustainability, safety, or respect for people, to be more than words. Yet day-to-day behavior often falls short. In this chapter, I will describe the one thing great managers do to ensure their subordinates fully internalize their organization's Core Values.

## CORE VALUES ARE COSTLY

**Core Values are difficult to adopt day-to-day because they represent short-term costs.** For example:

- **Sustainability:** Environmentally friendly products and machines usually have higher purchase costs.

- **Safety:** Workers must wear Personal Protective Equipment, which costs money, and follow procedures, which take time.

- **Respect for People:** Star employees must be disciplined like anyone else, with the risk of disgruntling them.

Core Values also come with long-term benefits. Sustainable companies enhance their image, leading to higher sales and reduced regulatory risks. Safe companies enjoy better workplaces, with lower turnover, higher-quality output, and more orderly, efficient operations. Learning to follow safety procedures also improves the ability to follow any procedure, leading to higher Operational Excellence. Companies that practice "Respect for People" or "Diversity" attract and retain talent more easily. However, **while the costs of Core Values appear immediately, their returns emerge only in the long term.** This dynamic fosters two behaviors: workers act lazily because benefits feel distant, and managers under deadline or cost pressure focus on short-term costs. As a result, employees hesitate to embrace Core Values, fearing punishment for incurring short-term costs.

For example, imagine a maintenance worker repairing a broken machine. They notice another machine nearby with moving parts, posing an injury risk. They might think of asking the line supervisor to temporarily shut it down, but anticipate the reply: production cannot stop because it would be too costly. To avoid reprimand, the worker proceeds without stopping the machine, risking personal injury. Of course, managers know that practicing Safety brings long-term benefits: fewer injuries, higher morale, and better-maintained machines. Yet in day-to-day operations, they feel only the immediate cost of stopping production. Likewise, maintenance workers feel the short-term risk of reprimand more acutely than the long-term benefit of safety.

**Good managers know employees often avoid Core Values out of fear of short-term penalties. By personally incurring these costs, managers signal that the costs are worth paying and that everyone is expected to follow suit.** A manager who puts on safety shoes before entering the plant sends a clear message: "Safety is a cost worth incurring. Safety is good for business." Conversely, managers who ignore safety gear signal the opposite: "Safety is a waste and should be minimized."

Managers who take the time to follow safety procedures send a clear message: "You won't be punished for doing the same." Conversely, managers who skip these procedures communicate an equally clear, but opposite, message: "I only spend time on actions that directly contribute to the bottom line, and you are expected to do the same."

## COST AS A SIGNAL

Diamonds signal commitment precisely because they are expensive. The costlier an action, the stronger the signal it sends.

Similarly, costly actions are essential for changing habits. Bad managers who rely on words to communicate Core Values fail because words are cheap, so their effect is limited. Conversely, good managers combine words with actions. **The costlier the action, the stronger its impact in internalizing Core Values.**

By cost, I mean time, money, or emotion. Purchasing high-quality Personal Protective Equipment is a financial cost; stopping production for ten minutes to discuss Safety is both a time and money cost.

Managers who do not value Core Values often try to minimize these costs, thinking that lower costs are better. But hiding the cost hides the importance of the action and misses an opportunity to influence subordinates positively.

**Good managers make costs visible, but in a thoughtful, non-transactional way.** Instead of saying, "We paid $15 each for the new gloves; you better use them," they might say, "We paid $15 each for the new gloves; it's a lot, but it's well-spent because Safety is that important."

The more visible and significant the costs, the more they signal the importance of Core Values. However, this does not mean inflating costs artificially: buying $30 gloves when $15 ones are sufficient would suggest poor judgment. The goal is transparency, not overspending.

## EXAMPLES OF COST AS A SIGNAL

**A16Z's fines.** Silicon Valley venture capital firm Andreessen Horowitz (A16Z) charges employees $10 per minute if they're late to meetings with entrepreneurs (their "customers"). This sends a clear signal that valuing time and respecting customers is a Core Value of the company.

**Amazon's doors.** In its early months, Amazon's CEO, Jeff Bezos, and his employees used wooden doors as desks due to cash constraints. The practice continued for years, even as resources became available. New employees asking about the desks would be told, "Here at Amazon, we look for every possible way to keep costs low and offer our customers the best price." This made the Core Value of frugality memorable from day one.

**DuPont's phone-at-the-wheel ban.** DuPont prohibited employees from using phones while driving. This costly signal prioritized safety over productivity: employees could have made calls during long drives, but were instead asked to focus on their well-being. This is a visible and memorable way to reinforce Safety as a Core Value.

## CULTURE IS CREATED BY GENUINE ANECDOTES

The three examples above illustrate not only the power of cost as a signal but also the importance of anecdotes in creating memorable anchors for a culture. Without such stories, even a strong culture risks fading over time.

## CULTURE IS CREATED BY VISIBLE COSTLY ACTIONS

**Culture is not made of perks and terminology but of time-consuming and cost-intensive rituals that are conspicuously perceived as worth it.**

## WHAT SHOULD BE THE UNCOMPROMISABLE CORE VALUES OF YOUR COMPANY?

This decision rests with Top Management, but here are some options worth considering:

- **Safety** is an excellent choice. Safe operations are cost-effective: less downtime, lower employee turnover, fewer insurance fees, reduced legal costs, and no need to replace injured employees with less experienced ones. In my experience, once Safety is internalized, related improvements naturally follow: a safe warehouse becomes orderly, workers who follow safety procedures also follow other procedures, morale rises, and so on.

- **Ethics** is another strong Core Value. Ethical behavior builds trust with candidates, suppliers, and clients, lowering recruitment, sourcing, and sales costs. Conversely, unethical actions can be extremely costly: a single rogue employee can incur millions in litigation, and unethical decisions can threaten a company's license to operate.

- **Excellence, Quality,** or **Customer Focus** are also excellent choices, for they are naturally aligned with what makes a great business. A personal favorite of mine is *Managerial Excellence.*

It is usually wise for a company to choose a Core Value that reflects its brand and competitive advantage. Examples include customer experience, reliability, speed, quality, or cost savings. However, avoid selecting too many. Usually, three or four is a good number.

## PREVENTING VIRTUE SIGNALING

In recent years, strong Core Values, especially Diversity and Sustainability, have sometimes devolved into virtue signaling. This isn't a problem with the values themselves, which are important and can be successfully upheld, but with superficial implementation. How can this be prevented?

The key is to make it clear that **employees are expected to perform on both Core Values and business outcomes: both are required, and neither alone is sufficient.** Failure in either leads to a negative performance evaluation, regardless of success in the other.

In my experience, this is the most effective way to prevent virtue signaling.

## THE NEED FOR UNCOMPROMISABLE PRIORITIES

"Building a great company requires that great decisions be made at all levels, not just the top. As a company grows, the number of decisions and the number of people making them proliferate. What to do? [...] The principles behind a decision are as important as the decision itself. I've observed that a sound decision is more likely when conversation and documentation are encouraged about the why and the what."

— *STRIPE'S BRIE WOLFSON*

Hence, the need for uncompromisable priorities: tools that help employees at all levels make decisions aligned with the organization's long-term goals, and that guide supervisors and managers to evaluate their subordinates' work in ways that reinforce the right principles.

## WHOSE ROLE IS IT TO DEMONSTRATE UNCOMPROMISABLE PRIORITIES?

Taking visible, costly actions to demonstrate the importance of Core Values is part of every manager's and supervisor's role. Ideally, this begins with the CEO. When the highest officer sets an example through visible, costly actions, it signals to the entire company that Core Values must always be followed, even when expensive or inconvenient.

Even if you are not the CEO, you can begin demonstrating your company's Core Values by taking visible, costly actions for your subordinates, aiming for a local shift in behavior. Success will depend on your skills and whether your superiors interact with your team in ways that implicitly encourage compromising Core Values for short-term gains.

If your superiors undermine your efforts, you may need to get them on board. Explain the principles in this chapter or show them these pages. If that fails, do not get discouraged, and keep your focus on improving the culture within your team. If you do a good enough job, its performance will soar, and you will get noticed.

## WHERE TO DRIVE CORE VALUES?

CEOs and Plant Managers have a superpower: they are the most visible people in the company or plant. Therefore, they have the most power to drive cultural change. If they hide in offices or conference rooms, they waste that superpower.

Make sure you spend regular time at your employees' workplaces. Best Practices #1 and #2 in Part Two of this book explain how to do this effectively.

## CULTURE IS THE TRACK RECORD

Leaders who think organizational culture is a set of concepts try to change it with words and inevitably fail. **Culture is not a set of concepts; it's a track record of which behaviors lead to personal gain and which are wasted effort.**

For example, when someone raises their hand, do they get heard, or do they learn it's pointless? That track record determines whether raising hands becomes part of the team's culture.

Defining and communicating Core Values alone doesn't change culture. It's only a first step. **Culture is changed by changing the track record**, and that requires actions, not words. Words can start and support the process, but only actions backed by words actually shape culture.

## SUMMARY

**Core Values are difficult to implement because they are costly: they incur short-term costs but deliver long-term benefits.** Even though the benefits outweigh the costs, employees need to trust that they won't be punished for bearing these short-term costs by a manager who only considers immediate results.

Core Values succeed when it is clearly acceptable to pay their costs. **Visible, costly actions allow a manager to send two crucial messages:** "The long-term benefits justify the short-term costs of practicing our Core Values" and "You will not be punished for incurring these costs, because you can follow my example."

**Culture is created through visible, costly actions, not perks or terminology. It is shaped by time- and cost-intensive rituals that are clearly perceived as worthwhile.**

**4**

---

# THE 4TH PRINCIPLE OF OPERATIONAL EXCELLENCE

## GOOD MANAGERS ARE OBSESSIVELY CONSISTENT IN HOLDING THEIR SUBORDINATES ACCOUNTABLE

I n this chapter, I discuss how to link individual outcomes to the performance of your subordinates.

When I mention rewards and punishments, I do not limit myself to raises, promotions, awards, or disciplinary actions. I include these, but also consider kind words, assignments to desirable or undesirable projects, letters of merit, opportunities for personal growth, and so on. Similarly, praises and reprimands are not only public displays of appreciation or disapproval but also one-on-one conversations.

Managers have a range of tools to apply individual outcomes to their subordinates' actions, and they should always choose the most appropriate.

Before we continue, let me clarify one thing: **applying individual outcomes to performance is not about squeezing every bit of productivity from employees.**

**It is about treating them fairly and giving them the chance to work where good work is valued and rewarded, and their efforts are noticed.**

Performance management is not about compliance or short-term output. **It is about preventing motivational losses so that long-term productivity can become a meaningful goal for employees.** The difference between squeezing productivity and treating employees fairly lies in setting humane objectives: ambitious *yet attainable* goals that do not force workers into self-destructive efforts.

This point will be further explored in the next chapter, "The Role of the Manager."

## GOOD MANAGERS ARE CONSISTENT

Once a good manager communicates a standard to their team, they consistently measure performance against it. They never apply double standards or make exceptions. They understand that doing so would compromise the integrity of the standard, making it pointless – just like a single hole can ruin an entire boat.

Bad managers are inconsistent in applying standards. They wrongly assume workers respond to the average application, whereas employees remember the extremes. **If a bad manager holds subordinates accountable nine out of ten times, they will remember the one time he didn't.** They will say, "But boss, Jack did the same last month, and you didn't care." Failing to enforce the standard even once opens the door to countless new transgressions.

## GOOD MANAGERS ARE CONSISTENT IN REWARDING GOOD WORK

Good managers look for opportunities to catch their subordinates meeting operational standards. When they see a job well done, they make sure to acknowledge it.

They do not need to praise employees every day, but when they do, they ensure it is clear that their attention is genuine. "Thank you, John, for doing such a good job. You've been excellent lately!"

Most managers understand that daily praise can lead to complacency, but bad managers respond by praising inconsistently, creating confusion and frustration. Subordinates may wonder, "Is good work not important anymore?" Conversely, good managers address complacency in high performers by extending evaluation timeframes ("I've measured your work daily, but since you've been consistently excellent, I'll switch to weekly evaluations") and by raising standards. The key is **never to compromise consistency, even when combating complacency.**

## CONSISTENT JUDGEMENT IS WELL PERCEIVED

Good managers understand that only inconsistent judgment or judgment on unclear objectives can be perceived as unfair. **Consistent judgment on clear, unambiguous objectives cannot be unfair.**

Inconsistent application of rules, including "good faith exceptions," invites thoughts such as "I've been judged unfairly," "This rule is unfair," "This rule is wrong," or "My manager has it in for me." All of these undermine future performance and team chemistry.

Consistently applying rules without exception keeps employees focused on how to achieve better results. A side benefit is that those who disagree with the rules will quickly quit or avoid joining, saving both the employer and themselves wasted time.

## GOOD MANAGERS CHOOSE APPROPRIATE REWARDS AND PUNISHMENTS

Managers have a wide range of tools to apply individual outcomes to their subordinates' actions: words of appreciation, letters of merit, one-time bonuses, promotions, assignments to better projects, training opportunities, honest feedback, verbal or formal warnings, disciplinary letters, and more.

Managers should select the most appropriate reward or punishment based on the magnitude of the consequence of the subordinate's action. A simple "thank you" may suffice for completing a minor objective, but it would be inadequate for an employee who improved a production process, saving the company hundreds of thousands of dollars per year. In that case, a sizable financial bonus and a letter of merit should be the minimum.

The principle is to match individual outcomes to the consequences of objectives achieved or violations of Core Values, so subordinates feel fairly treated relative to their performance.

**In general, people accept being treated differently if it is fair. What they cannot tolerate is being treated unfairly.**

## GOOD MANAGERS NEVER REWARD TRESPASSING CORE VALUES

Good managers never reward employees who violate core values, even if their actions yield results. They understand that celebrating success achieved by breaking core values signals that such behavior is acceptable, or even expected.

## GOOD MANAGERS NEVER REWARD EFFORT (THEY REWARD RESULTS)

**If managers reward effort, subordinates will eventually focus on showing effort rather than delivering results.** Good managers may acknowledge effort, but they never reward it. They might say, "I noticed that you worked very hard, but you did not achieve the results I asked for, and that is what matters."

## GOOD MANAGERS SET HIGH STANDARDS

Entrepreneur Ben Horowitz noted, "In good organizations, people can focus on their work and have confidence that if they get their work done, good things will happen for both the company and them personally."

Employees rightly expect that satisfactory work will lead to positive outcomes, such as occasional raises or promotions. Managers who set low standards face a problem: some employees meet the standards, but the company cannot justify extra compensation because insufficient value has been created. Conversely, **good managers set targets high enough that achieving them produces a windfall that can be shared across the team.**

## GOOD MANAGERS ARE CONSISTENT IN NOTICING WHEN STANDARDS AREN'T MET

Good managers understand that even their best subordinates sometimes produce subpar work. They also know that failing to acknowledge this can demotivate top performers. Ignoring substandard work may signal that the work isn't important or that the manager doesn't care. **Double standards are always harmful to subordinates, even when they appear to favor them.**

Instead, good managers address subpar work in a motivating way. They do not say, "Your work is terrible." They say, "Your work has always been good, but in this instance, you didn't meet the standard. What happened?"

Good managers recognize that new employees often arrive highly motivated, but they lose motivation when faced with situations where the manager "doesn't care" or applies double standards. **The manager's role is not to actively motivate employees, but to prevent demotivation by ensuring fairness and consistent attention. Their focus is on avoiding motivational losses.**

Demotivated people are not incapable of seeing the value in meaningful work; they are people who, at some point, did not receive the upside they deserved. **Motivated and demotivated employees are both responding correctly based on past experiences. The manager's job is to create new, positive experiences.** Whenever managers fail to be fully consistent and fair, subordinates lose motivation – often, the company's most valuable asset.

## GOOD MANAGERS OBSESS ABOUT CONSISTENCY

Years ago, I worked with an operations manager who had a problem: mechanical parts were scattered across the warehouse floor, making it difficult to walk without stepping on something. For months, he repeatedly told employees to store parts properly. Yet, they never did so.

The issue was that the warehouse was too large, and the manager was too busy to consistently enforce standards. So, he decided to focus on a single point and obsess over it. He chose the area next to a machine. In a stand-up meeting, he told employees that this area must always be clear. He instructed them to clear it immediately and didn't leave until it was done.

For the next month, he visited the warehouse multiple times a day, first checking the machine area. If it wasn't clear, he would stop whatever he was doing, find the nearest employee, remind them of the rule, and stay until it was followed. He obsessed over it.

After one week, employees learned the machine area had to stay clear. After two weeks, they noticed it was easier to walk and parts were easier to find. After three weeks, the magic happened: employees began clearing other areas on their own.

**The manager succeeded by focusing on a small area, obsessing over it, and letting employees see the benefit of the change.**

**This is the magic of obsessive consistency. Once workers realize they can change faster than the manager, and that positive results follow, they will change.**

Good managers leverage the power of obsessive consistency.

## GOOD MANAGERS AIM TO REACH CRITICAL MASS

Some experts say an action becomes a habit after 21 consecutive days; others say it happens once everyone in a room performs it simultaneously. Both emphasize the importance of reaching a critical mass, whether over time or socially.

Consistency is essential for two reasons. First, it helps achieve the critical mass needed for actions to become habits in our brains. Second, inconsistency kills habits. The first time an employee performs below standard without consequence, it invites a repeat and signals to others that underperformance is tolerated. It doesn't matter whether this is true—what matters is the perception created.

**Because good managers understand the importance of critical mass, they limit the magnitude of change at any one time.** Instead of asking subordinates to adopt five new habits at once, they focus on one. This prevents attention from being spread too thin and reduces the likelihood of missing instances where a habit is not followed.

They also restrict the number of people adopting a new habit simultaneously. Rather than requiring an entire building to adopt a habit at once, they focus on one or two teams. This ensures no bad habit goes unnoticed and no good habit unreinforced. Employees watch how colleagues are treated; if they see lapses go unaddressed, they learn they can do the same. By obsessing over a single habit within a small group, good managers prevent such lapses and reinforce desired behaviors.

## THE TRICKY PART

The tricky part of the Fourth Principle of Operational Excellence is that it doesn't start working the moment you apply it. It begins to work only when there is no instance in which it isn't applied. You must have faith that once critical mass is achieved, change will occur —but not before.

## CHAPTER SUMMARY

Good managers reinforce change consistently by focusing on a single new habit and a small group of people at a time. They make the time and energy for this because they recognize that consistency is the most important attribute of a good manager.

Great companies promote management consistency and reinforce it through deliberate, often costly trade-offs by leadership, ensuring everyone understands its importance.

Good managers are fair, not loyal. **Employees often say they want loyal bosses, but what they truly want is fairness.** Loyalty to everyone at all times is impossible, but fairness to everyone every time is achievable.

**5**

———————

# PARADIGM SHIFTS

The Four Principles of Operational Excellence introduce four paradigm shifts:

- The First Principle shifts from "understanding objectives is the subordinate's responsibility" to "assigning unmistakable objectives is the manager's responsibility."

- The Second Principle shifts from "succeeding at a delegated task is the employee's responsibility" to "great managers set their employees up for success."

- The Third Principle shifts from "management has to be efficient" to "signals must be costly to be effective."

- The Fourth Principle shifts from "making the right decisions is a matter of pragmatism" to "whether a decision is right is determined by how it influences the future behavior of employees."

Discussing these paradigm shifts helps convey the principles more effectively than simply defining them.

**6**

———

# THE ROLE OF THE MANAGER

Before moving on to the Eight Best Practices, it is worth spending a few pages on the role of the manager.

## GOOD MANAGERS ARE PROACTIVE

*"Lead proactively, do not manage reactively."*

*– Keith Rabois*

Good managers do their job well today because yesterday they planted the seed for effective management: clarity.

**Bad managers make decisions based on their immediate impact. Good managers make decisions based on how they will influence the future behavior of their subordinates.**

## LEVERAGE

Doing the work of a subordinate is a low-leverage action: ten minutes of your time produces only a slightly better output than ten minutes of theirs.

Training, by contrast, is high-leverage. Spending 1% of your time training eight subordinates to improve their output by 1% each gives you 8× leverage.

The higher the leverage of your activities, the greater your contribution to your team's effectiveness. Avoid spending time on low-leverage tasks and focus on high-leverage ones: long-term decisions, training, improving clarity, and preventing motivational losses.

## OVERCOMMUNICATION

**You've only truly communicated something when it feels like you've overcommunicated it.** Managers often hesitate to repeat themselves for fear of questioning their subordinates' intelligence. Therefore, the expectation to overcommunicate must be made explicit, so that politeness doesn't undermine effectiveness.

Patrick Lencioni defines overcommunication as when "Employees understand how they contribute to the success of their organization. They do not spend time speculating on what executives are really thinking." I agree with him.

Don't hesitate to repeat yourself. It's worth it.

Oh, and by the way: overcommunication must also be costly; a footnote in a slide deck won't suffice. Show up in person.

## MAKING THE IMPORTANT CONSPICUOUS

In discussing the Four Principles of Operational Excellence, great emphasis has been placed on making the important conspicuous: ensuring that everyone knows the important elements—Core Values and their uncompromisability, personal objectives, and the fact that individual outcomes will inevitably follow performance—and that everyone knows that everyone else knows it too.

**As a manager, your main tasks are to make the important unmistakable and conspicuous, and consistently reward people based on results against their personal objectives, and their stewardship of Core Values.**

## COMMUNICATING MEANING

Employees work best when they are engaged in meaningful work and understand its significance.

Almost any job can be meaningful, as it enables others to enjoy products and services. For example, in a memorable 1960 speech to Hewlett-Packard employees, cofounder David Packard said: *"In those areas where we are making instruments, we are supplying about one-third of the country's total requirements [...] it indicates that we have a responsibility, in that we are making a very major contribution to the total technical effort of this country. Your efforts are not only worthwhile, but you are doing something really significant in terms of total technical effort. You have seen photographs of important scientific work being done, and those photos include HP instruments. Those of you who visit the labs of our customers find our instruments are being used in very important work, the advancement of science, the defense of our country, and many other areas. So, don't overlook our responsibility."*

You can do the same as Mr. Packard: explain to your subordinates how your organization's products impact the lives of their users.

Do not assume they already understand this, and do not assume that explaining it is an insult to their intelligence. **People need to be explicitly reminded of the value of their work, even if they already know it, and this reminder should come regularly, so that on a bad day, frustration has no fertile ground to grow.**

Managers and supervisors are responsible for emotionally conveying the meaning of work: what feelings do your organization's products create for their users, directly or indirectly?

**As a manager, your job is to help subordinates understand the meaning of their work and to ensure they, in turn, help their own subordinates do the same.**

## GOOD MANAGERS ARE AWARE OF HOW EMPLOYEES ADAPT

**Good managers understand that employees respond primarily to the incentives, explicit or implicit, that their experience has trained them to expect.**

Therefore, good managers act not for immediate results, but for how subordinates will adapt to those actions. Every time they fairly apply individual outcomes to performance, employees adapt in the right direction. Every time they fail to do so, employees adapt in the wrong direction.

For this reason, good managers are obsessively consistent in holding subordinates accountable, and they do so without remorse, precisely because they set humane objectives and have been unmistakably clear about what those objectives represent.

## GOOD MANAGERS ARE IN FOR THE LONG RUN

Good managers understand that employee turnover is costly, both personally and operationally. Personally, it takes time to know someone, build trust, learn to manage them effectively, appreciate their work, and integrate them into the team. Operationally, it takes time to recruit, hire, and train a new employee and for them to become effective in their role, team, and company.

Therefore, good managers work to eliminate as many sources of frustration as possible that might drive employees to leave:

- **Useless effort:** Employees lose motivation when they expect a reward or acknowledgment for their work and do not receive it, either because the manager is too busy or because objectives were not clear enough, leading to misunderstandings about what constitutes satisfactory results. Motivation is also lost when employees produce outputs that ultimately do not contribute to team or company success (e.g., spending a week on a report that no one reads).

- **Unfairness:** Employees lose motivation when they perceive unfair treatment, such as seeing a lower-performing employee paid more, or noticing that someone skipping effortful procedures is not reprimanded. Sometimes this resentment is misplaced—for instance, when the better-paid employee is delivering value that isn't immediately visible—but even then, it usually stems from the manager failing to clearly and conspicuously define what a good result looks like, so that agreement on contributions can be established.

The First, Second, and Fourth Principles of Operational Excellence focus on setting objectives with such clarity and rewarding them with such consistency that the two sources of motivational loss described above do not affect your subordinates.

Similarly, good managers are effective at addressing the root causes that lead employees to leave the organization due to burnout:

- **Chronic overwork:** As noted in the introduction, occasional periods of increased workload are normal and indicate a healthy business. Chronic overwork, however, is a symptom of structural problems.

- **Unrewarded overwork:** Overwork that brings rewards (a bonus, a sense of accomplishment, etc.) usually does not cause burnout, except in extreme cases. In contrast, overwork without rewards leads to burnout, often quickly. This includes when overwork is potentially rewarded, but the performance threshold is so high that achieving it becomes either overwhelming or unattainable.

Therefore, good managers ensure they do not cause chronic overwork among subordinates, and when occasional workload spikes occur, they appropriately reward employees for the extra effort.

Note that I used the word "cause" rather than "ask." Managers cannot hide behind excuses such as, "I never asked them to work overtime; they just happen to do so." Chronic overwork is a symptom of a poorly structured business, insufficient staffing, inadequate training, or ineffective management, all of which are the responsibility of management.

## THINGS BAD MANAGERS DO

Bad managers spend time on unimportant tasks or on work that their subordinates could handle.

They take pride in their problems, valuing the appearance of busyness and effort over real effectiveness.

They project their issues onto subordinates, seeing them as problems rather than opportunities.

They do whatever it takes to achieve short-term results.

They are pragmatic, willing to compromise Core Values if the payoff seems large enough.

They are more competent than their subordinates at the subordinates' own jobs, because they do not train them enough.

## THINGS GOOD MANAGERS DO

Good managers obsess over identifying which objectives and behaviors are critical for the long-term success of the organization, focusing everyone's attention on them and rewarding employees for turning them into reality.

They ignore the noise and focus on the signal in everything they do: what they observe, punish, and reward.

Good managers are obsessive stewards of Core Values.

## 10 WAYS TO KILL MOTIVATION AS A MANAGER

1. Ask your people to do things, then never check whether they actually did them.

2. Ask your people to work more carefully, then punish them for being slow.

3. Never explain your decisions; let your team assume you had no valid reasons.

4. When someone shows motivation, give them no opportunities to act on it. Let it vanish.

5. Set conservative goals so that even if your subordinates achieve them, there isn't enough windfall to reward them.

6. When someone does something good, wait a few days to acknowledge it. Make them doubt whether their effort was worthwhile.

7. When someone notices a problem, make them work overtime to fix it, even if they didn't cause it. Next time, they'll stay silent.

8. When someone underperforms, don't tell them until the yearly review. Let them believe they're on track for a raise until it's too late.

9. When delegating, never check in early. If they misunderstand something, let them waste effort before correcting them.

10. When delegating, only reveal part of your requirements. Then be disappointed when they deliver exactly on what you told them but not what you didn't.

7

———

# CONCLUSIONS OF PART I

Operational Excellence is about selecting, reinforcing, and sustaining the mental patterns in your team that foster autonomous action aligned with the organization's long-term objectives.

**Setting unambiguous, individual, and rewardable objectives, de-risking delegation, taking costly actions to signal important principles, and being obsessively consistent are the core areas to focus on.**

This is the best way to prevent motivational losses and avoid circumstances that could dilute both your authority and your organization's Operational Culture.

# PART II

———

# BEST PRACTICES

In the first part of this book, I presented the Four Principles:

1. Good managers set unambiguous, individual, and rewardable objectives.

2. Good managers always explicitly assign full accountability together with tasks and objectives.

3. Good managers demonstrate priorities with visible, costly actions.

4. Good managers are obsessively consistent in holding their subordinates accountable.

In the second part of this book, I will present the Eight Best Practices that transform those principles into **visible actions**.

They are called Best Practices because they must be *practiced* week after week for the organization to benefit. Just as physical fitness requires ongoing training rather than one-time effort, Operational Excellence demands continuous practice of the following eight activities.

**1**

---

# BEST PRACTICE #1:

## MANAGEMENT WALKS

If a manager does not know what is happening in Operations, they cannot manage them properly. If workers do not see their manager spending time where Operations take place, they will not trust that management is effective. For these reasons, managers must spend time where the work they oversee is done.

The Toyota Production System (TPS) calls this *Genchi Genbutsu* ("Go and See"). According to the TPS, to truly understand a situation, one must go to the real place where work is performed.

However, gaining practical knowledge and being seen gaining it are only two of the three reasons good managers go to the workplace. The third is taking visible actions.

**Decisions made in an office stay there; managers can only influence how subordinates work by translating decisions into visible actions at their workplaces.**

To do this, good managers use Management Walks.

## MANAGEMENT WALKS

Management Walks are regular occasions when a manager physically goes to where subordinates work. This includes not only direct reports but, more importantly, everyone further down the hierarchy. Even a CEO, to be an effective manager, should spend at least an hour a month on the factory floor, observing workers and interacting with them through visible actions that signal the company's priorities.

Other Operational Excellence systems have similar practices, known as "Gemba Walks," "Line Walks," or "Observations."

## WHAT HAPPENS DURING A MANAGEMENT WALK?

During a management walk, the manager performs the following set of steps:

1. The manager walks near where workers are operating and silently observes them, following all required procedures (e.g., safety rules such as wearing a helmet) to set a good example and show that no one is exempt.

2. The manager looks for something good, something bad, or something they do not understand.

3. If they notice something good, they personally thank the worker. If they see something they do not understand, they ask the nearest worker for an explanation with humility and openness, avoiding making suggestions until they fully understand why things are done that way.

4. If they notice something bad, they approach the worker violating company procedures, rules, or Core Values (or the closest worker, if what violates the rules is an object). They politely wait to interrupt until it is safe to do so and ask why the person is acting that way, assuming nothing until they have gained a full understanding of the context.

5. If there is a reasonable explanation for having violated the rules or procedures, the rules or procedures must be rewritten to reflect the circumstance. Otherwise, the behavior cannot be excused. The manager must remind the employee of the proper way of working and ask for **immediate** compliance to confirm understanding and help form the habit. Finally, they thank the worker for their time and cooperation.

A manager should never let any behavior that violates rules, procedures, or Core Values go unnoticed. **Either the rule or procedure must be rewritten, or the worker must acknowledge that they should not have acted that way. There is no grey area or one-off exception; letting something pass once is how exceptions become the new norm.** Good managers never allow that.

Begin by being open to the possibility that the rule is wrong, but once you determine it isn't, apply it with categorical inflexibility. If the worker had a valid reason to act as they did and the rule must be rewritten, immediately ordering the change is a Visible Action showing that exceptions cannot exist. A rule is either always right or it is wrong, nothing in between.

## WHO PERFORMS MANAGEMENT WALKS?

Everyone does, with different frequencies.

- Top management, including the CEO, should conduct at least one a month.

- Managers should conduct at least one a week.

- Supervisors should conduct at least one a day.

This may seem like a lot, but it is essential for achieving Operational Excellence. Operational Excellence flows from clarity and visible examples, and Management Walks are the ideal tool for the latter.

## SHOULD WORKERS PERFORM WALKS TOO?

In a company where Operational Excellence is fully internalized, yes.

However, if your company is still at the beginning of this journey, only managers and supervisors should perform them. Only after line workers have internalized the concept from their managers can they take on Walks themselves.

When workers do Walks, they either observe their teammates in their own workplace or in adjacent areas such as nearby production lines or warehouses. Observing teammates promotes peer accountability, while walking in nearby areas encourages cross-pollination of Best Practices and prevents complacency. Seeing the same workplace every day can make chronic problems seem normal.

## WHAT TO LOOK FOR DURING A WALK?

There are three types of situations to watch for during a Walk: conditions, behaviors, and moods. Drops of oil on the floor are an unsafe condition, a worker walking the shop floor without safety shoes is an unsafe behavior, and workers appearing tired or rushed all the time are an unsafe mood.

Bad managers only call out bad conditions and behaviors—situations that are unsafe or wrong according to rules, procedures, standards, and Core Values. Good managers, during Management Walks, call out both good and bad conditions and behaviors, and they also pay attention to moods.

*The following page contains a few non-exhaustive lists of common conditions, behaviors, and moods to look for.*

## SOME CONDITIONS TO LOOK FOR

- Is there any non-labeled container, machine, tool, or button?

- Is any object placed where it could fall easily?

- Are the walkways encumbered?

- Are there tools out of place?

- Are the shelves messy?

- Is the space dirty?

*Note that everything in this page applies not only to the factory floor but also to administrative offices, retail shops, salespeople's cars, etc.*

## SOME BEHAVIORS TO LOOK FOR

- Are the workers using the wrong tools or misusing the right ones?

- Are they breaking safety or operational procedures?

- Are they walking or standing in unsafe areas?

## SOME COMMON MOODS TO LOOK FOR

- Are the workers frustrated or in a bad mood?

- Are they focused or distracted?

- Are they tired or sleepy?

- Are they complacent?

- Are they rushing?

A more comprehensive checklist of conditions and behaviors to look for will be presented in the next chapter, called "Best Practice #2: Audits."

## LOOK FOR BOTH THE GOOD AND THE BAD

Behavioral theory suggests that positive reinforcement (praising or rewarding good behavior) can be more effective for forming habits than negative reinforcement (reprimands or punishment).

This does not mean negative reinforcement should be avoided. For the sake of consistency (the Fourth Principle of Operational Excellence), a manager cannot ignore violations of rules, procedures, standards, or Core Values. To maximize effectiveness, both positive and negative reinforcement must be used. Good managers watch for both the good and the bad and act on each.

## PROVIDING IMMEDIATE FEEDBACK

When managers see a good or bad condition or behavior, they should immediately interact with the relevant worker. Praise or reprimands are most effective when delivered right after the observation. (Of course, if an immediate interruption would compromise safety, managers should wait for the first safe opportunity.)

If the observation involves behavior, the manager addresses the worker who performed it. If it involves a condition, the manager interacts with the employee closest to where it was observed. For example, if a manager sees a sharp tool left on the floor near an unattended worktable, they should interact with the worker assigned to that table. And if they see a sharp tool left on the floor in a generic spot, they should interact with the closest worker, even if that person is merely passing by.

It is essential to show that **rules, standards, and Core Values are a shared responsibility.** Holding peers, subordinates, and superiors accountable is everyone's responsibility. If this seems excessive or unrealistic, I still remember an anecdote from my time at a Fortune 100 company. A customer's CEO was climbing the stairs of our headquarters on his way to an important meeting, while one of our maintenance workers was descending. The worker, in his uniform, stopped to remind the CEO, in his suit and tie, to hold the handrail for safety. Did the CEO get offended? Not at all. Impressed by our culture, he not only completed the product deal he came to sign but also hired us to improve the culture at his own company.

**Anyone can and should call out violations by any person, including executives, and, if the violation occurs on company premises, even customers and contractors.**

## ALWAYS CRITICIZE BEHAVIORS, NEVER PEOPLE

**When calling out something wrong, managers should focus on the behavior, never the person. Criticizing someone as a person usually provokes anger, frustration, or defensiveness, which can lead to ignoring the feedback or even spreading demotivation.**

People are generally more open to feedback on their behavior, especially if they feel the manager has tried to understand their perspective. That's why managers should take a few seconds to observe before speaking and ask, "Why were you doing that?" before giving feedback. Asking first provides valuable insight and makes the worker more receptive.

## ASK QUESTIONS THE RIGHT WAY

Managers should never ask questions arrogantly, as this only produces negative results. Instead, they should ask with the benefit of the doubt, acknowledging there may be a reason for the subordinate's behavior, while remaining firm in rejecting all excuses.

The wording of questions is crucial. For example, asking, "What would you change here?" often receives silence or indifference, whereas "If you were the line manager here, what would you change?" usually elicits thoughtful and enthusiastic responses. **When asking questions, give subordinates the authority to answer them.**

## A SCRIPT FOR A GOOD MANAGEMENT WALK

*The manager walks on the factory floor. He looks around and sees a worker performing maintenance on a machine without a helmet.*

*He observes for a few seconds, then approaches, signaling his intention to speak. (It's better not to interrupt abruptly unless there is imminent danger, as sudden interruptions can cause reactions or loss of concentration.)*

**Manager:** "Hi. Thank you for taking care of our machines." *(Start with a genuine thank you related to a real reason.)*

**Manager:** "I've noticed you aren't wearing a helmet. Is there any reason?" *(Even if the rule is clear, the manager seeks to understand the worker's perspective and make them receptive to feedback.)*

**Worker:** "Oh, sorry, it's just a two-minute task."

**Manager:** "Two minutes might be enough to get injured. Helmets must always be worn inside the factory. Your safety is important." *(Reinforce that rules and Core Values like safety are never to be compromised.)*

**Manager:** "Please wear a safety helmet." *(Request immediate compliance.)*

**Worker:** "Okay."

*The manager waits while the worker puts on the helmet, showing that his words are always followed by action.*

**Manager:** "Thank you for wearing the helmet. You're an important team member, and keeping you safe benefits everyone." *(Always thank the worker.)*

**Manager:** "Is there anything on your mind you'd like to discuss?" *(Every interaction is an opportunity to gather information.)*

## A SECOND SCRIPT FOR A GOOD MANAGEMENT WALK

*The manager walks on the factory floor. He notices a few machinery components on the floor where they shouldn't be. He approaches the closest worker, raising a hand to catch attention.*

**Manager:** "Hello. I've noticed some components blocking the walkway. Is there any reason they are here?"

**Worker:** "John just left them temporarily. He'll pick them up in an hour when the rest are ready."

**Manager:** "I understand, but the walkway must be fully accessible at all times." *(The manager is inflexible, treating Core Values as non-negotiable priorities.)*

**Manager:** "Could you please put the components in their proper place?"

**Worker:** "I'll tell John to do it as soon as possible."

*Seeing that John is not nearby, the manager says:*

**Manager:** "Please do it yourself now. It's important. Safety is everyone's priority." *(This prevents the components from being left out and reinforces peer accountability.)*

*The worker reluctantly moves the components, while the manager observes or helps. Once done, the manager thanks him:*

**Manager:** "Thank you for helping keep the plant safe and respecting the rules. They exist for a reason, and we should never compromise them."

*Remember: the point of Management Walks is not only to spot errors but also to reinforce procedures and Core Values with visible, tangible actions, like spending a few minutes ensuring rules are followed.*

## COMMUNICATING STANDARDS AND PRIORITIES

**Management Walks, like all performance management, are about communicating standards and priorities clearly and practically.**

Managers should always keep this in mind, never compromising on standards or priorities, *especially* during a Walk, when their actions and priorities are most visible.

## A FINAL NOTE

If you have a reputation as a poor manager, you may perform a Management Walk correctly yet get poor results, because workers won't be receptive to someone they don't trust.

If trust is lacking, build it first. However, do not look for the kind of trust that comes from being a "good friend." Instead, build trust as a capable leader who improves the working lives of others. Off-sites, dinners, or events may be fun, but they do not increase confidence in your management competence. Instead, spend more time on Management Walks, focusing on asking questions and understanding the challenges of your workers' jobs, *while resisting the urge to offer suggestions unless asked.*

Do this at least twice a week for two months, and you will notice people becoming more open and receptive.

## ACTION POINTS

1. Create a schedule for your Management Walks: book a 30-minute slot once a month if you are Top Management, once a week if you are a manager, and once a day if you are a supervisor.

2. If you are a manager of managers, meet with your subordinates to have them implement Management Walks in their routine. During the meeting, set clear objectives for what constitutes a successful Walk (First Principle of Operational Excellence) and derisk the delegation (Second Principle). Accompany them on their first Walk, coaching them and taking visible, costly actions to reinforce the principles (Third Principle). Finally, schedule a follow-up meeting to review results and maintain accountability (Fourth Principle).

**2**

---

# BEST PRACTICE #2:

## MINI-AUDITS

Mini-audits are scripted Observation Walks. Instead of walking into an area and making free observations, the observer uses a checklist. Examples appear later in this chapter.

Note that **mini-audits are different from the large, complex, compliance-focused audits companies perform annually. Mini-audits are lightweight and meant to be done weekly or at least monthly,** *not by a specialized auditor but by the manager of the area.*

The manager enters the area with a single-page checklist in hand. For each checklist item, they check whether it is being observed. If it is, they mark it as complete and compliment a nearby worker. If not, they mark it as incomplete and interact with a nearby worker as they would during an Observation Walk.

At the end, the checklist is sent to the area supervisor and the local HSE manager (even if only part of the audit covers safety). The results are displayed visibly, for example, on a wall chart, so progress can be tracked.

Before covering how audits are performed, by whom, and how often, let's first look at an example checklist.

## AN EXAMPLE AUDIT CHECKLIST

The checklist below is for illustration only. Each company should create its own to suit its specific processes. Ideally, select 10–30 items and fit them on a single-page checklist that is easy to print and carry.

Remember to create checklists for both your plants/warehouses and your offices.

## UNSAFE HABITS:

- Is anyone missing their PPE (Personal Protective Equipment)? *Sub-checklist: helmet, glasses, gloves, mask, earplugs/muffs, protective suit, safety shoes, harness, sensors, etc.*
- Is anyone performing maintenance on electrically powered installations without Lock-Out-Tag-Out (LOTO)?
- Is anyone using the stairs without using the handrail?
- Is anyone not wearing a seatbelt?
- Is anyone taking a shortcut?

## LACK OF FOCUS:

- Any signs of distraction?
- Any opposing priorities?
- Any signs of frustration?
- Is anyone multitasking?
- Any signs of rushing?
- Any signs of fatigue?

*Note: In some contexts, it's okay if someone is not focused all the time. Use nuance and discernment.*

## DISORDER:

- Is 5S observed? *(5S is a workplace organization method based on five Japanese words: "Sort," "Set in Order," "Shine," "Standardize," and "Sustain.")*
- Is any emergency exit blocked, or is any fire extinguisher inaccessible?
- Are walkways missing clear boundaries?
- Is there any unprotected sharp surface?
- Is any item in a precarious position?
- Is any area excessively dirty?
- Is any walkway obstructed?
- Is any tool out of place?
- Is the room too dark?
- Is any label missing?
- Is the floor wet?

## TOOLS:

- Is any tool out of place or left in a precarious position?
- Is any tool inappropriate, deteriorated, or broken?
- Is any tool being misused?
- Is any tool unergonomic?

## PROCEDURES:

- Do workers have the relevant work permits, if any?
- Is any worker not following the procedures?

**SELF-AUDIT:**

- When I observed something wrong, did I get the relevant worker(s) to take *immediate* corrective actions?

- Did I observe both the good and the bad?

You may have noticed that most items focus on safety. This is intentional. As explained in the chapter on the Third Principle, safety is a leading indicator of Operational Excellence.


## WHO PERFORMS AN AUDIT?

Audits should be conducted both by Line Managers, who "own the area" and have the technical knowledge to observe most effectively, and by all managers above them, so they spend time on the work floor and become familiar with the operations of their organization.

Once more, let me repeat the importance of conducting audits not only in manufacturing and logistics areas but also in offices.


## HOW OFTEN SHOULD AUDITS BE PERFORMED?

Line Managers should perform an Audit at least once a month, in addition to conducting at least one Management Walk per week. Higher-level managers should perform at least one Audit per quarter and at least one Management Walk per month.

Audits always complement Management Walks; they are not alternatives. The checklist used in an Audit helps ensure key conditions, behaviors, and moods are observed, but it can also constrain attention and prevent the auditor from noticing issues outside the checklist. This is why performing both Management Walks and Audits is essential.

It may seem like a lot, but this book is about achieving Operational Excellence, not just attempting it.

## WHEN AUDITS FAIL

In my experience, Audits fail when they become inconsequential: when they are treated as a checklist to go through and nothing more.

To be effective, performing Audits should be a personal objective for anyone required to do them, with the same importance as output-related objectives.

As discussed in the chapter on the Second Principle of Operational Excellence, when giving your subordinates Audit objectives, set a clear standard for what constitutes a successful Audit and how it will be evaluated.

## ACTION POINTS

1. Create an Audit checklist for the office or plant where your subordinates work.

2. If you are a Line Manager or Supervisor, book a 30-minute monthly slot in your calendar to perform the Audit. If you are a Manager, schedule a meeting with your subordinates to assign them regular Audits, setting clear expectations in line with the First and Second Principles of Operational Excellence and consistently evaluating their performance according to the Fourth Principle.

3. Book a 30-minute slot three months from now to review your auditing process and make any necessary adjustments. If you are a Manager, invite your subordinates to join.

# 3

## BEST PRACTICE #3
### WEEKLY MEETINGS

To understand the impact of Weekly Meetings on shaping company processes, let's look at them from the attendees' perspective.

- Whether the meeting starts on time and how late arrivals are treated signals to attendees whether time is considered an important resource in the organization.

- The first item on the agenda indicates what should remain top of mind for the rest of the week.

- Mentioning the organization's Core Values during the Weekly Meeting signals whether they are still relevant.

- The tradeoffs explicitly highlighted by the manager during decisions or when communicating previously made decisions inform attendees about the tradeoffs they can make in their daily work.

- If a Core Value or standard is compromised during the Weekly Meeting, attendees will conclude that they can compromise it too.

## WEEKLY MEETINGS ARE OPPORTUNITIES FOR REINFORCEMENT

**The primary function of Weekly Meetings is to reinforce the organization's Core Values and Operational Culture.**

If something is discussed during the meeting, it is likely important. If it is not discussed, attendees will assume it is not (or at least, that is the conclusion they will draw).

Good managers understand that organizational culture can erode and that repeating the importance of a metric or Core Value does not imply doubting their subordinates' intelligence. **People need reminders, not because in their absence they forget, but because in their absence, they believe their content doesn't matter anymore.**

When a decision is made during the meeting, any criteria compromised in trade-offs signal to attendees that they are expected to make the same compromises in the following week. For example, if a manager decides it is acceptable to sacrifice quality to meet a deadline, attendees will internalize the message "It is okay to sacrifice quality to meet targets" and may compromise quality in their own future decisions.

## WEEKLY MEETINGS ARE TOOLS TO DISPERSE DOUBTS

Even if the manager and company consistently uphold Core Values, employees may still doubt whether they can embody them when doing so would compromise short-term output. This is particularly true for those employees who, in the past, have worked for a boss or company that never allowed short-term results to be sacrificed.

Good managers dispel these doubts by using Weekly Meetings to reaffirm each week that the company's and team's Core Values remain unchanged and that employees are still expected never to compromise them.

**Good managers know that, no matter how often Core Values have been emphasized in past meetings, if they are omitted in a given Weekly Meeting, doubt will resurface.** Attendees may wonder: "Why didn't the manager mention the Core Values while outlining this week's priorities? Does it mean we can or should compromise them to meet this week's targets?"

## WEEKLY MEETINGS ARE TOOLS FOR CONSPICUOUSNESS

Weekly Meetings are an exceptional communication tool because the manager can speak to the entire team at once. **Each attendee knows that any expectation set during the meeting is heard by everyone else.**

For example, if the manager says that John must complete a key task this week and everyone else on the team is expected to support him when asked, John will feel more confident seeking help.

Setting expectations in a way visible to everyone is a powerful way to influence others' actions. Compare two workers: one who knows what needs to be done and believes their colleagues know it too, and another who knows what needs to be done but thinks others are unaware or uncommitted. The first is more likely to ask for help and hold colleagues to operational standards, regardless of whether they truly know or embrace what must be done.

**Good managers communicate not only to ensure subordinates understand and embrace what needs to be done, but also to make sure everyone knows that everyone else understands and embraces it.** Weekly Meetings are an ideal channel for this.

The primary focus of Weekly Meetings is communication: first and foremost, of Operational Culture, and secondarily of whatever the manager needs to convey to the team that week.

## WEEKLY MEETINGS ARE NOT ABOUT TAKING DECISIONS

In an ideal world, no major decisions are made during Weekly Meetings. Instead, decisions are taken in ad-hoc meetings, where only those whose input is required are invited.

However, for some teams, it makes sense to make decisions during Weekly Meetings, particularly if most decisions require input from most team members, or if it is logistically advantageous to hold a single meeting (for example, if the manager is located in a different office and visits the team only once per week).

In such cases, Weekly Meetings should be divided into two phases: communication and decision-making, in that order. Otherwise, decision-making can dominate the meeting, leaving the communication phase rushed and poorly absorbed. The chosen order also sends an implicit message: what is discussed first signals the real priority.

## WEEKLY MEETINGS ARE NOT TO SHARE PROGRESS BUT TO CREATE IT

Weekly Meetings are often used for progress updates, where each team member reports on what they did last week and what they plan to do this week.

This can be a waste of time if it amounts to one-way reporting, or highly productive if used to anticipate obstacles and drive progress. For example, the manager can help subordinates prioritize tasks or ask about obstacles and risks, offering guidance on how to address them.

**A Weekly Meeting is ineffective if attendees leave in the same position they were when they arrived. It is effective when they leave with a clearer, more actionable to-do list than when they entered.**

## WHAT HAPPENS DURING AN EFFECTIVE WEEKLY MEETING?

### AT THE BEGINNING

The manager thanks attendees for arriving on time, explaining that punctuality is a sign of respect for each other's time and work. This accomplishes several things: it makes people feel their effort to arrive on time is valued, encourages them to continue arriving on time to avoid feeling like outsiders, and clarifies that punctuality is required not out of the manager's rigidity, but out of respect for their colleagues' time.

### THE AGENDA

The first topic on the agenda should be an update related to one or more of the organization's Core Values. For example, the manager might begin the Weekly Meeting by asking if anyone has observed unsafe behavior or conditions (if Safety is a Core Value) or if there have been any delighted customers (if Customer Satisfaction is a Core Value). I call this a "Core Value Review."

The bulk of the meeting should focus on communication, primarily from the manager to the team. The manager conveys all necessary information while using every opportunity to reinforce Core Values and standards.

Any decisions should be made only after all communication has taken place.

## HANDLING DISCUSSIONS

It is normal for heated discussions to arise during meetings, as long as they focus on issues rather than personalities. If a comment targets someone personally, the manager should immediately redirect it toward behavior. For example, if an employee says, "John is lazy" because it takes multiple emails to get him to handle requests, the manager might respond, "You mean John is slow to respond to internal requests?" This approach achieves several outcomes: John is more likely to respond constructively rather than defensively, and the feedback becomes more precise, highlighting specific areas for improvement.

If the manager consistently reminds subordinates that "here, we discuss issues, not personalities" whenever a personal critique arises, the team will learn to frame their comments appropriately within a few weeks. The manager must not allow even a single personal comment to pass without correction, **not even once**. Doing so would undo all prior effort, and the team would quickly revert to destructive feedback.

## HANDLING DECISIONS

If two participants disagree during the meeting, the manager should let them resolve it, possibly outside the meeting, to avoid wasting everyone's time. Similarly, if multiple participants have a prolonged disagreement on a decision affecting the whole team, the manager should step in as the final arbiter.

Some managers hesitate to do this to avoid displeasing anyone. They should remember that people rarely get angry when a decision they dislike is made, but they do get angry if it is made without hearing them out. As long as the manager collects input from everyone with an opinion and ensures they feel heard, they can confidently decide without provoking personal anger (though subordinates might still feel frustration).

While listening to their team, managers must be careful not to rely on their own assumptions to interpret what is said. True listening involves understanding not just the words spoken but, more importantly, the assumptions behind them.

## AT THE END: GETTING ACTIVE COMMITMENT

Before the meeting ends, the manager must ensure every participant is committed to completing their assigned tasks, even if they disagree with them. Weekly Meetings should follow the "disagree and commit" model: participants voice concerns and feel heard, but ultimately support the final decisions.

If the "disagree and commit" model seems unrealistic, it is usually because previous managers failed to truly listen. Subordinates generally accept decisions if they feel heard; disagreement often stems from the perception that their concerns were ignored.

Proper listening can take time. For this reason, only necessary participants should attend the meeting to keep the group small. Managers should also meet beforehand with individuals likely to have concerns, allowing time to listen effectively.

A common risk is a supervisor who disagrees with a decision and, therefore, neglects to communicate it to their teams, creating surprised reactions when their team eventually learns about it. Hence, the importance of gathering, during the team meeting, an active commitment from all attendees to communicate the decision to their teams.

Moreover, communication must be framed constructively. A message such as, "Management decided X, and we have to live with it," fosters discontent. Instead, supervisors should convey support, for example: "We decided X; this isn't ideal due to concerns A and B, which I raised during the meeting, but for reasons C and D, X is in everyone's best interest."

One of the worst outcomes of team meetings is passive commitment, where participants neither agree nor disagree. They carry out assigned actions, but without enough commitment to ensure success. This makes accountability difficult, as subordinates technically fulfilled their tasks but insufficiently. Passive commitment equals passive sabotage.

To prevent this, **great managers require active commitment from every participant.** They ask, "What will you do after this meeting to carry out your assigned tasks?" Conversely, bad managers would be content with, "Will you do this?" which might not be enough.

**Great managers demand conflict** (encouraging concerns), **then commitment** (ensuring everyone promises what they will do), **and finally results** (holding everyone accountable). Missing any of these three steps might be fatal to later execution.

Therefore, **before the meeting ends, the manager has to ensure that every participant walks out the door committed to doing whatever task was assigned to them during the meeting, even if they did not agree with it.**

## ACTION POINTS

1. If you do not already hold regular Weekly Meetings with your subordinates, schedule one immediately.

2. Book a 15-minute slot immediately after each of the first three meetings to re-read this chapter and reflect on what went well and what could be improved.

4

——————

# BEST PRACTICE #4
## ONE-ON-ONE MEETINGS

*"People who think one-on-one meetings are a bad idea have been the victim of poorly designed ones."*

— *BEN HOROWITZ*

One-on-one meetings are a powerful tool for gathering intelligence, reinforcing priorities, assigning accountability, and reviewing performance in an intimate setting. They are so effective that every manager should hold them with each direct subordinate at least once every other week.

**One-on-one meetings should last at least half an hour, even if it seems there is nothing to discuss. This is because there is always something to discuss.** If it appears otherwise, the manager may need to improve at asking questions or handling silence. The most useful information often emerges after a long, awkward pause, when the subordinate finally voices what they would not mention earlier. This is usually the most important information.

## CONDUCTING ONE-ON-ONE MEETINGS

The first time a manager holds a one-on-one meeting with a subordinate, they should take time to explain the purpose of these meetings. The manager should clarify that they will occur weekly, but they are not instances of micromanagement. On the contrary, ideally, they will be the only management-initiated contact during the week, aside from Weekly Team Meetings and Management Walks. Because the manager uses the weekly meeting to ensure the subordinate is aligned on priorities, the subordinate is free to act independently the rest of the week. Of course, there may be additional contact, for example, during project-specific meetings or subordinate-initiated conversations.

Weekly one-on-one meetings are tools to gather intelligence and reinforce priorities, Core Values, and accountability, not for micromanagement.

Here is an example structure. First, the manager thanks the subordinate for coming and asks if any urgent issues need discussion. This clears concerns that might occupy the subordinate's attention. However, urgent issues should take no more than half the meeting; if a single issue requires more time, an ad-hoc meeting can be scheduled.

Second, the manager asks for high-level progress updates on assigned tasks and projects. Updates should not go into detail; their purpose is to identify whether the subordinate is stuck or off course. During progress updates, the manager must not accept excuses. There is a difference between "this came up, so I am taking care of it" (good) and "this came up, so the project will be delayed" (bad). The first demonstrates ownership and a solution; the second shows passivity and missed objectives.

Ensuring objectives are met on schedule and according to specifications should remain the top priority for both manager and subordinate. If focus is lacking, it is the manager's job to restore alignment.

During updates, the manager should encourage the identification of potential problems by asking questions such as, "If the project falls behind schedule, what might cause it?" This is a *pre-mortem*, in contrast to a post-mortem, which occurs after project completion. Follow-up questions such as "So, if we do X and Y, can we be certain the project won't be delayed, or could there be other sources of delay?" ensure all necessary actions are surfaced.

Once progress updates are complete, there should be remaining time. If not, the manager either allocated too little time or allowed the discussion to dwell on unnecessary details.

**The rest of the meeting should focus on gathering intelligence:** What problems might the team face? What personal issues affect the atmosphere? Does anyone need support? What important matters remain unspoken? One effective approach is to respond to a non-informational answer with silence. Subordinates often feel compelled to fill the pause, revealing information they would not have shared otherwise. The silence should last at least 30 seconds; if no response occurs after one minute, the manager can prompt gently: "Is there anything else I need to know about the team?"

**If the manager properly focuses on gathering intelligence, reinforcing priorities, and unlocking progress rather than micromanaging, subordinates will, within a few weeks, begin to look forward to weekly one-on-one meetings.**

In fact, whether your subordinates look forward to one-on-ones is the best indication of whether you're holding them in a way that's helpful to them rather than in a way that's helpful to you.

## GOOD QUESTIONS TO ASK

In my experience, the following questions are very effective in surfacing important information: "On what pending issues is there no progress?" "What are you scared of?" "What are we scared of, as a team or as a company?" "What should be on my to-do list as a manager, but isn't?" and "What should be on our to-do list as a company, but isn't?" The purpose of these questions is not to collect advice, but to gather intelligence.

In his book *The Hard Thing About Hard Things*, Silicon Valley executive Ben Horowitz suggests the following questions for one-on-one meetings: "If we could improve in any way, how would we do it? What's the number one problem with our organization? Why? What's not fun about working here? Who is kicking ass in the company? Whom do you admire? If you were me, what changes would you make? What don't you like about the product? What's the biggest opportunity that we're missing out on? What are we not doing that we should be doing? Are you happy working here?"

**It is critical that, after asking a question, the manager allows the subordinate to answer freely, without interrupting or criticizing. Otherwise, that may be the last time the subordinate shares useful intelligence.**

After the subordinate answers, the manager may offer their own perspective on the topic. However, they should never criticize or imply criticism toward the subordinate who provided the answer.

## ACTION POINTS

1. Schedule a one-hour one-on-one meeting with each of your direct subordinates this week or next. Do not schedule multiple meetings at once with the same subordinate; instead, use a rolling schedule: at the end of each meeting, set the date for the next one.

2. After completing the first round of meetings, reread this chapter to review what went well and what could be improved.

**5**

---

# BEST PRACTICE #5

## BRIGHT SPOT ANALYSIS

Bright Spot Analysis is a powerful tool for generating ideas to improve your Operations. I first learned about it from Dan and Chip Heath. It involves three steps: identifying the top performer in your area, understanding what they do differently, and seeing if others can do the same.

## THE FIRST STEP: IDENTIFYING THE BRIGHT SPOT

Good managers routinely ask themselves the following questions:

- "Who is the best-performing person in my team?"
- "Which is the best-performing team in my unit?"
- "Which is the best-performing line in my factory?"
- "Which is the best-performing factory in my company?"
- "Which is the best-performing company in my industry?"

These questions may refer to overall performance or to specific tasks (for example, "Who is the best person in my team at ensuring projects are completed on time?"). Both can offer valuable lessons.

## THE SECOND STEP: UNDERSTANDING THE BRIGHT SPOT

Once the Bright Spot has been identified (an employee, a team, a line, a plant, or a competitor), the manager studies its behavior to see if it is caused or enabled by traits, procedures, or environmental conditions that can be replicated in other areas under their control.

Good managers routinely ask themselves two questions:

1. Is there anything the Bright Spot does that makes it exceptionally effective and could be replicated elsewhere in the organization?

2. Is there anything about the environment in which the Bright Spot operates that makes it exceptionally effective and could be replicated elsewhere in the organization?

The second question is often overlooked, as people tend to attribute exceptional behaviors to individual personalities. In reality, most behavior is shaped by the environment, including incentive systems, management, and team or organizational culture. These factors are largely replicable, though doing so requires time and effort.

For example, once a team has been identified as the Bright Spot, the manager should examine its goals, incentives, managers, and culture. Could any of these explain their exceptional performance?

*Pro tip: Don't just ask "who" is the Bright Spot; also ask "when." For instance, which day last week were you most productive? What happened that day? Is there anything under your control worth replicating?*

## THE THIRD STEP: REPLICATING THE BRIGHT SPOT

Once the cause of the Bright Spot has been identified, the manager should try to replicate it across the organization, if and where it would be appropriate to do so.

For example, if the Bright Spot is a team following a procedure that no other team uses, and it makes sense for others to adopt it, the manager should roll it out across the teams.

*The process for implementing new procedures is described in the third part of this book.*

## NO CHERRY-PICKING

Cherry-picking is the process of forming an opinion of a person or group of people based on one single aspect of their performance rather than on their overall results.

When performing Bright Spot Analysis, managers should avoid cherry-picking performance data and focus on overall performance. If a team or individual excels in one area, such as production output, but performs poorly overall, for example, in quality, would you really want to replicate their procedures just to increase speed?

## SIDE EFFECTS

Every intervention, practice, or procedure has side effects: the time, energy, and money required for implementation, and the potential loss of morale in those told that "the way they were working before was wrong."

Managers using Bright Spot Analysis must consider, before the third step, whether any new practice or procedure would deliver enough benefits to outweigh its side effects, leaving a margin of safety for possible hidden costs.

## CHOOSE SOMETHING THAT WORKS, NOT SOMETHING THAT MAKES SENSE

When choosing a procedure or factor to replicate, limit yourself to things that have been proven to work, rather than ideas that merely make sense.

Copying practices that already work is called bottom-up adaptation and has a high success rate. Implementing untested ideas is called top-down adaptation and usually fails, especially after taking into account survivorship bias (failed experiments are forgotten, while only successes are remembered).

There are two reasons for this. First, most ideas need repeated refinement; copying something that works means adopting a solution already refined, whereas untested ideas will likely require further adjustments before succeeding. Second, most initiatives have hidden side effects, often larger than the obvious benefits. Proven practices have usually revealed these side effects over time, while untested ideas can bring unexpected problems.

## DARK SPOTS

The sister practice to Bright Spot Analysis is Dark Spot Analysis, which works similarly:

1. The manager identifies an individual, team, or line that is underperforming.

2. The manager investigates the root cause of the underperformance and works to address it.

3. If successful, the manager replicates the solution to prevent the same issue from recurring under their management.

The insights from step three can also be shared across the company, if appropriate.

## ACTION POINTS

1. Schedule a 30-minute slot in your calendar for the Bright Spot Analysis. *(This is a low-priority task; the Action Points from previous Best Practices take higher priority.)*

2. When the time comes, re-read this chapter and apply its contents.

3. Schedule a follow-up 30-minute session to perform another Bright Spot Analysis.

**6**

---

# BEST PRACTICE #6

## STANDARD OPERATING PROCEDURES

 *"When companies choose chat first, they revert to an almost oral tradition."*

— *DAVID H. HANSSON*

In all kinds of organizations, writing down procedures, rules, standards, and Core Values is important for three reasons. First, it makes them permanently available, so anyone can check them at any time and know how they are expected to act. Second, it makes them conspicuous; following written traditions means you don't have to justify your actions to others or risk being wrong. Third, it allows for the fair application of individual outcomes.

A company that relies solely on oral tradition will face many problems. Employees may not know what to do, receive conflicting guidance on tradeoffs, or justify selfish behavior by saying, "What he said wasn't clear" or "But I was told otherwise."

By contrast, Standard Operating Procedures (SOPs) form most of a company's written tradition. SOPs are sheets detailing the most crit-

84

ical procedures employees might encounter. They are regularly reviewed and stored in an easily accessible location for anyone who might need them.

SOPs serve three main purposes. First, they provide any worker performing a business-critical task with a reference to follow. Second, they offer an objective standard to verify whether anything went wrong. Third, when operations change, such as adding new hardware or updating a procedure, SOPs allow other procedures to be checked for possible collateral effects.

## THE STRUCTURE OF SOPS

Standard Operating Procedures are bundles of sheets (or their digital equivalent) that include at least the following elements:

- **A title.**

- **A unique identifier,** used to reference and locate the procedure. It is usually a number or alphanumeric string.

- **Some steps** for workers to follow. They should also include any required guidance to avoid common mistakes.

- **A date of last review or modification.**

- **An expiration date,** indicating when the procedure must be reviewed. Setting an expiration date, usually 6 or 12 months after the last review, ensures procedures are regularly evaluated. This is critical as the environment constantly changes (e.g., new machines, new supplies, or loss of experienced staff).

- **A purpose,** clarifying why the procedure exists and helping reviewers identify "zombie procedures" that are no longer needed.

- **A responsible role,** indicating who is accountable for writing and reviewing the procedure and ensuring a competent review occurs when required.

- **The signature** of the person who wrote or last reviewed the procedure, confirming responsibility.

- **A list of roles to be informed of modifications.** For example, a procedure to operate a machine might require review by the maintenance team before changes are implemented.

## MANAGEMENT OF CHANGE

In companies far from achieving Operational Excellence, procedures often contain only a title, a list of steps, and sometimes a signature. They neglect Management of Change (MoC): the checks needed to ensure that whenever something in the procedure's environment changes, the procedure is updated accordingly, and that whenever the procedure is about to be changed, any necessary changes in its environment are considered.

Therefore, all SOPs should include the additional components listed above. Otherwise, they will function only until they inevitably fail.

## CONTRACTORS

Written SOPs are especially useful for managing contractors. Make sure you don't limit SOPs to direct employees, forgetting about contractors.

## THE STORAGE OF STANDARD OPERATING PROCEDURES

Standard Operating Procedures must be stored in a location easily accessible to anyone who needs them. Typically, this is a binder with transparent sleeves, each holding a single procedure. Except in the smallest premises, multiple copies of the binder should exist so workers don't have to walk long distances to consult them. A system must ensure that whenever an SOP is changed, the update is replicated across all binders.

SOPs are often also maintained as digital files to facilitate edits and reprints. Still, a paper version should be kept, especially in non-office premises, unless every worker always has a device to access the latest procedure. Paper may seem inefficient, but it has advantages and is often more likely to be consulted: consider that most books are still sold in paper form, even though eBooks are widely available.

## JOB DESCRIPTIONS

Job descriptions are a particular type of SOP. Broadly, the requirements for a position and its tasks describe part of the procedures that Human Resources and managers must follow to hire or promote someone.

Job descriptions are better described not as a set of skills ("is good at sales") but as a set of objectives they must be able to competently execute ("must be able to grow sales by 20%"). The latter gives a much clearer idea of what hiring should screen for.

Job descriptions are the responsibility of the manager overseeing the role. In large organizations, HR should support the task, but the manager's input is essential.

Every position should have a written job description that meets the SOP requirements listed a few pages ago, including an expiration date, signature, and purpose.

Some of the best managers I know also prepare documents listing expected behaviors and those to avoid for the position, circulating them internally either privately with the role-holder or publicly by posting them visibly in the office or plant.

## META-PROCEDURES

There should also be procedures for managing procedures: at a minimum, one for creating SOPs, one for updating them, and one for reviewing them.

## ACTION POINTS

If you have the authority to create procedures, follow these steps.

1. Write the three meta-procedures described above, clarifying which areas of competence should have procedures and who is responsible for writing each.

2. Schedule a 30-minute meeting with the people responsible for writing procedures. Review this chapter with them and assign them the task of writing the procedures they are responsible for. If your company already has some SOPs, ensure that old SOPs are checked and rewritten if necessary, and that the need for additional SOPs is evaluated.

3. Schedule follow-up meetings to track the progress of procedure writing.

4. Once procedures are written, ensure the appropriate people review them: HSE, Line Supervisors, relevant technical specialists, and anyone directly involved in using or managing the procedures should be informed and given a chance to review.

5. Delegate the task of printing and distributing the SOPs.

6. Assign each Manager and Supervisor the task of reviewing each procedure with the affected personnel.

SOPs are a complex topic, and the action list above may not be exhaustive. Your industry likely has additional requirements. Use your judgment, follow the Four Principles of Operational Excellence, and consult an expert if needed.

7

―――――

# BEST PRACTICE #7
## PROACTIVELY SURFACING PROBLEMS

You might have heard of a concept called *Just in Time*. Many business schools describe it as the idea of having components arrive at the production line exactly when needed, reducing the costs and handling time of storing them in a warehouse first.

This is only partially correct. It is true that handling components twice (first from the delivery truck to the warehouse, then from the warehouse to the production line) and renting storage space are unnecessary costs that do not add value to the customer. However, that is not the main advantage of Just In Time.

Warehouses act as buffers, protecting against supply volatility. For example, if a warehouse holds enough components, production can continue even if the delivery truck is late. A company with a buffer (say, enough components for a week) won't see a one-day delay as a problem, so no one takes steps to ensure timely delivery. If the truck were eventually a week late, production would stop, and the company would be unprepared. Conversely, a company without a buffer treats even a one-hour delay as a problem and acts immediately to ensure the truck arrives on time. This makes its operations much more robust and efficient.

**Buffers hide problems until it's too late. Just In Time (and other techniques that reduce buffers) surface problems so they can be solved before it's too late.**

Just In Time is about removing buffers to surface problems.

## THE RED ROPE

Toyota production lines used to have a red rope hanging from the ceiling, called the *Andon Cord*. Any worker was instructed to pull it whenever they noticed a problem in the production process, such as a defect. Pulling the rope would immediately stop production.

Anyone who has worked in a plant knows how costly stopping production can be. At Toyota, it happened every time a worker, any worker!, noticed a problem and pulled the rope. What a way to ensure problems are solved immediately, rather than getting lost in suggestion forms!

The red rope is not only a brilliant implementation of the third Principle of Operational Excellence (demonstrating priorities by taking costly actions) but also a perfect way to align incentives toward solving problems immediately.

## PROBLEM SOLVING

The two examples above, Just in Time and the Red Rope, introduce the topic of this chapter: implementing problem-solving techniques and designing incentives to ensure they are used proactively, before serious problems arise, rather than reactively.

Escalating problems to upper management or experts is extremely slow for two reasons. First, it takes time for the issue to reach the person who can solve it and for them to act. Second, even starting the escalation can be slow, as line workers often hesitate to "create problems" and may wait hours, days, or weeks before raising the issue.

This is clearly problematic. **Problems grow to the size they need for us to acknowledge them. An organization that is slow in acknowledging problems will find itself with big problems.**

The alternative is to establish systems that tackle problems as soon as their first symptoms appear, or even before. There are two complementary approaches: decentralized problem-solving and measuring leading indicators.

## DECENTRALIZED PROBLEM SOLVING

Decentralized problem-solving involves providing tools and setting expectations so that line workers can solve problems at the lowest competent level.

## TOOLS

Line workers and line managers have a wide range of tools and techniques for solving operational problems.

The most famous is perhaps Six Sigma. While it cannot be applied to all problems (most of its methods work best in contexts with Gaussian-like distributions), it is a valuable tool for line workers and managers to solve problems themselves in a structured way.

Another well-known tool is the "5 Whys," in which workers ask themselves the cause of a defect multiple times, typically five, using each answer as the basis for the next question. For example:

1. Why did my teammate injure himself? Because he tripped on a cable.

2. Why was the cable on the floor? Because it connected a tool to a plug on the other side of the room.

3. Why wasn't the tool plugged into the closest side of the room? Because there was no plug there.

Asking three "why" questions in a row revealed both the root cause, the lack of plugs, and the solution: have an electrician install a plug on that wall.

In my experience, the correct number of iterations is not five or any fixed number, but rather enough to ensure that addressing the problem will prevent a similar incident from happening again. In general, **a problem is truly solved only when the corrective action taken answers "Will this prevent the same problem from occurring again?" positively.**

Bright Spot Analysis and Dark Spot Analysis (Best Practice #5) are excellent tools for solving problems proactively.

## EXPECTATIONS

Many organizations understand the need for decentralized problem-solving and provide tools for line workers, but few also set the expectation that workers should actually use them. To some managers, this might seem obvious ("We gave them the tools; of course, they are expected to use them"). In reality, unless expectations are explicit and linked to personal outcomes, tools will often go unused.

Moreover, if a manager communicates that workers should solve problems themselves but then punishes, even subtly, anyone for doing so, the team will receive the opposite message: you are not really supposed to solve problems yourself. Here, "punish" is used broadly: even a disapproving look or eye roll counts.

Of course, there are times when escalation is appropriate. Clear procedures or rules of thumb must define which issues should be escalated and which solved locally.

**Managers must both provide problem-solving tools and consistently reinforce the expectation that workers use them autonomously. The effectiveness of decentralized problem-solving will always be limited by the weaker of these two factors.**

## LEADING INDICATORS

Leading indicators are a powerful tool for identifying problems before they occur. Here's a practical example from workplace safety.

In 1931, U.S. safety manager Herbert Heinrich observed a pattern in factory incidents. For each serious injury, there were many minor injuries; for each minor injury, numerous accidents caused no injury. These exact numbers were later disproved, but the principle holds: for every death, there are many serious injuries; for every serious injury, many minor injuries; for every minor injury, several "near misses" (such as a brick falling from the roof but hitting no one); and for every near miss, numerous unsafe behaviors (e.g., a worker walking without a safety helmet) and unsafe conditions (e.g., a sharp edge near a walkway).

These relationships can be represented as a pyramid, as shown below.

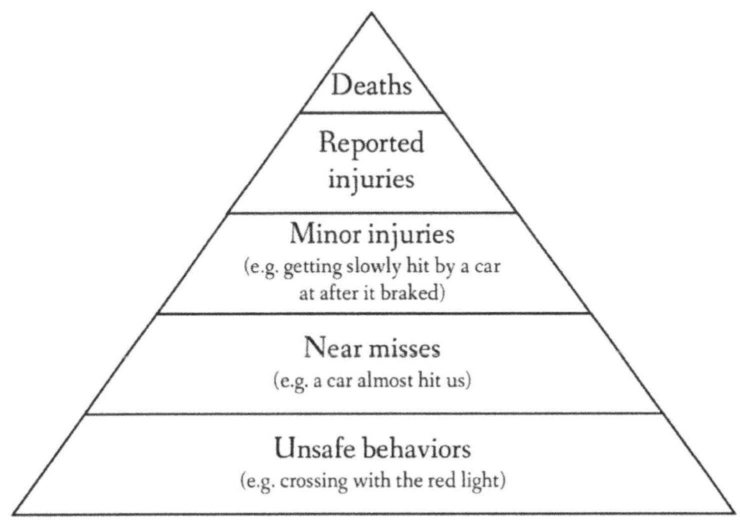

Let's do a thought experiment. Imagine a company recorded one workplace death four years ago, one three years ago, one two years ago, and zero last year. Can we conclude that the company has become safer?

| Time | 4 years ago | 3 years ago | 2 years ago | Last year |
|---|---|---|---|---|
| **Workplace deaths** | 1 | 1 | 1 | 0 |

No, we cannot. Perhaps the plant's actual safety level predicts 0.75 deaths per year, and last year, employees were simply lucky. There might be another death or two next year. The sample is too small, and **trends measured at the top of the pyramid are too volatile to be predictive.**

Now consider a second scenario. In the same company, 25 employees were injured four years ago, 30 three years ago, 15 two years ago, and 5 last year. Can we conclude the company has become safer?

| Time | 4 years ago | 3 years ago | 2 years ago | Last year |
|---|---|---|---|---|
| **Workplace deaths** | 25 | 30 | 15 | 5 |

Perhaps, but we cannot be certain. While the sample is now large enough to reveal more reliable trends, other factors could invalidate the results. For example, management might have covertly asked employees not to report injuries starting two years ago. It is also possible that operations causing minor injuries improved, while those posing rare but fatal risks, like electrical maintenance, did not. Finally, **trends measured in the upper levels of the pyramid lack insight into rare but catastrophic threats.** Employees may now be less likely to suffer common injuries, but could still face high risks from infrequent hazards, such as fires.

Now imagine that random observations in the same company showed that four years ago, 50% of employees wore safety helmets where required; three years ago, 80%; two years ago, 90%; and last year, nearly 100%.

Can we conclude that the company became safer? Most likely, yes. The sample size is much larger, so randomness has less impact. Moreover, there is a clear correlation between consistent safe behavior and overall workplace safety. Since most incidents result from unsafe behaviors, the workforce is now safer.

Trends measured at the base of the risk pyramid are more reliable because of larger samples and fewer assumptions. Indicators at the top, by contrast, have a major limitation: they only measure events that have already occurred, which is why they are called lagging indicators.

Organizations and individuals that rely on lagging indicators tend to be reactive, acting only after a negative event occurs. In contrast, indicators at the bottom of the pyramid (leading indicators) can reveal risks before they materialize. Companies and individuals using leading indicators are proactive, acting to prevent negative events.

For example, a company that increases safety training only after a workplace death is almost certain to experience at least one such death. But a company that responds when it notices employees not following safety guidelines can prevent all deaths.

**Measuring trends at the base of the pyramid enables proactive prevention, whereas measuring trends at the top keeps us reactive, responding only after problems occur.**

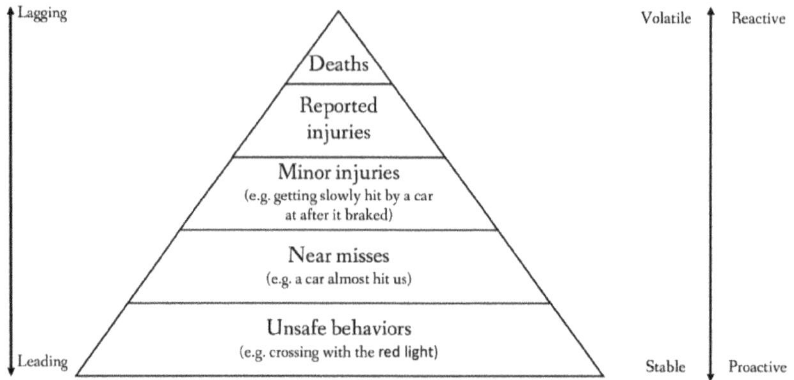


## USING LEADING INDICATORS

To effectively use leading indicators, managers must at least partially tie performance rewards to them rather than solely to lagging indicators. (Performance rewards include not only promotions and bonuses but also recognition, positive feedback, or even disciplinary actions.)

When harmful events are less frequent than positive ones, there is a risk of over-optimization: employees may become complacent during a lucky streak without incidents and take unnecessary risks. This makes it crucial to reward leading indicators, such as the number of employees wearing safety helmets, alongside lagging indicators, like the number of injuries. Without this, workers might optimize for the wrong metrics, such as skipping helmets to save a few seconds.

**By linking rewards and consequences to both leading and lagging indicators, the frequency of negative events increases, causing the incentive to optimize for the frequent small profits to disappear.**

Let's explore this with an example. A sales manager whose compensation is tied to sales (a lagging indicator) will focus on hitting the numbers for the current quarter. Any extra time will go toward making a few more calls or sending a few more proposals. They will prioritize small, quick clients over larger accounts that might take months to close, squeezing short-term profits while potentially harming long-term client relationships. In extreme cases, they might even be tempted to sell defective products or products that offer no real benefit to the customer.

Conversely, a sales manager whose compensation is tied to leading indicators, such as client satisfaction (predicting repeat sales), sales training attended (improving future sales), and thorough customer research and qualification (improving client quality and profitability), is more likely to generate strong long-term results.

When I introduce the pyramid of risk and leading indicators, people grasp the concepts easily. Yet in practice, a common mistake occurs: organizations measure leading indicators and pay attention to them, but fail to tie them to individual outcomes. If poor performance on a leading indicator has no consequence for the employee, behavior will not change.

As the pyramid chart illustrates, only the top half of the pyramid is inherently linked to physical harm. To ensure employees change behavior, emotional or career consequences must be tied to the indicators at the base of the pyramid.

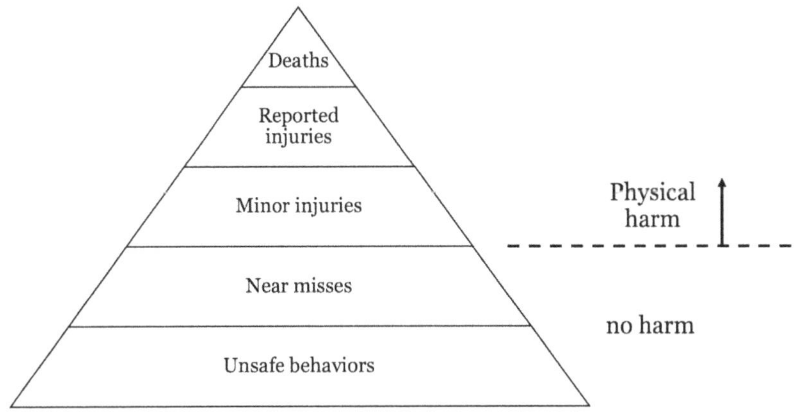

## SOLVING PROBLEMS WITHOUT USING SHORTCUTS

Problems are resolved only when their root cause is addressed. If a problem is fixed without addressing its root cause, the cause will generate new problems. Shortcuts are often the quickest path to a repeat of the same problem.

**Good managers insist on solving root causes, not just superficial problems. They do not reward those who tackle symptoms without addressing the underlying issue.**

## INCIDENT INVESTIGATIONS

Incident investigations are a particularly effective problem-solving tool. Triggered by safety, quality, or ethics incidents, their goal is to identify root causes.

While necessary, incident investigations are not sufficient on their own. They address problems that have already occurred, but cannot prevent issues that have yet to manifest. Therefore, they should be used alongside the other tools described in this chapter.

Incident investigations are conducted by an ad hoc committee formed immediately after the incident. This may happen formally or informally. More severe incidents require more formal procedures, but all incidents must be investigated. Lightweight procedures are essential to allow rapid investigation of minor incidents without bureaucratic delays. The Five Whys technique is a good example of such a procedure.

**The effectiveness of an incident investigation depends on the level of the highest-ranking person involved.** For consequential incidents, such as severe injuries, recalls, or harm caused by rogue employees, it is advised that the CEO or the highest local manager (e.g., Plant Manager) participate. While they are not expected to conduct the investigation directly, they should at least initiate it and be informed of the results. Their involvement is a costly and effective signal of the investigation's importance and facilitates information gathering and implementation of corrective actions.

The investigation should conclude with a written report answering three questions: what happened, what was the root cause, and what should be done.

Incident investigations are not about blaming individuals, though negligence must be addressed. Their purpose is to identify root causes and prevent recurrence.

## FRUSTRATION INCIDENTS

Traditionally, incident investigation is limited to safety incidents and, sometimes, quality incidents. I argue it should be extended to frustration incidents: moments in which an employee becomes frustrated as a result of interacting with a manager, colleague, or procedure.

Frustration incidents are fantastic signals of a root problem that, if left unaddressed, will erode the engagement of your workforce.

I suggest you treat frustration incidents as any other type of incident: worthy of triggering an investigation (though, of course, it doesn't have to be a formal one).

## CHAPTER SUMMARY

Companies with excellent operations deploy a variety of problem-solving tools and consistently reinforce the expectation to use them.

They act on incidents and declining leading indicators, with systems in place to address the root causes of both past and emerging problems.

## ACTION POINTS

1. Schedule a meeting with your HSE or Quality manager to implement an incident investigation procedure. Ensure a Standard Operating Procedure is documented. If procedures already exist, use the meeting to review whether they are applied consistently and effectively.

2. Identify relevant leading indicators for the areas you manage. Assign someone, possibly yourself, the responsibility for measuring and improving them.

3. Ensure that the next time decisions are made or problems addressed, it is done at the lowest competent level.

**8**

---

# BEST PRACTICE #8
## VISUAL AIDS

**V**isual aids include posters, labels on hardware, barriers, and any other form of visual communication designed to guide or remind those who see them. They provide visible, tangible reminders of what is important, even when the manager is absent. Moreover, **they serve as an indisputable, objective reference for standards and objectives: if a visual aid has been displayed for a month, no one can claim they didn't have the opportunity to see it. Assigning accountability will be easier.**

If I had to summarize the first three Principles of Operational Excellence in one sentence, it would be: "Make sure the important cannot be misunderstood." Visual aids are a key Best Practice for this, along with Observation Walks and Audits (which provide hands-on feedback), Weekly and One-on-one Meetings (occasions to restate what matters), and Standard Operating Procedures (another form of objective reference, though they must be actively consulted and cannot be "pushed" in front of people when needed).

The four most common forms of visual aids are posters, poster charts, labels, and barriers.

## POSTERS

Posters are large prints displayed on office, walkway, factory, and warehouse walls. They typically depict or describe rules, standards, priorities, and Core Values. For example, a warehouse poster might remind workers of safety rules, while an office poster might reinforce that "Environmental Sustainability" is a Core Value.

**Some managers dismiss posters, believing their subordinates already know the content. They forget that communication isn't complete when a message is first said; it is complete when it cannot be forgotten or misunderstood.** No message is clear enough to justify skipping a poster. Moreover, posters provide a visible, objective reference that spoken words alone cannot. A worker cannot claim, "You didn't say that!" when the message is posted on the wall.

As a rule of thumb, if no Core Value or Standard is displayed at least once on every office floor, factory floor, canteen, and warehouse, your company needs more posters. (Multiple Core Values or standards can share a single poster.)

## POSTER CHARTS

Poster charts are posters that track the evolution of one or more key metrics over time. They differ from normal charts in two key ways: they are displayed in a location visible to all workers in a given area, and their message is clear enough to be read at a glance. **Their primary function is not just to inform workers of trends but to keep key outputs of their job top of mind at all times.**

The best poster charts have titles large enough to be seen from 2–3 meters away. This allows workers to be reminded of what matters without stopping, and it reassures them that others have seen it, too.

As a rule of thumb, every factory or office worker should either work in front of a poster chart or pass one while walking from their workstation to the toilets.

## LABELS

Labels are small pieces of paper, fabric, plastic, or similar material attached to or placed near critical hardware. For example, a label might explain what happens if a button is pressed, identify the purpose of a key, or indicate the contents or hazards of a container (e.g., "inflammable"). Labels can also serve as directional panels, such as arrows pointing to emergency exits.

Great companies use labels extensively. Every critical button, tool, container, shelf, pathway, lever, valve, and indicator is clearly labeled. **Labels are not meant to compensate for inexperience; they protect against fatigue, rushing, and other conditions that might cause even competent operators to make mistakes.**

Some labels also improve efficiency. For instance, factory workers may use colored stickers on tools and matching locations on their worktables, ensuring each tool has a designated place and speeding up operations when many tools are involved.

A particular type of label is floor markings indicating walkways or separate areas. These serve three functions: they keep workers out of prohibited zones, such as forklift paths; they guide them safely to their destinations; and they delimit areas for parts and equipment, keeping walkways clear and reducing the risk of injuries.

## BARRIERS

Barriers are physical devices that restrict movement, preventing workers from entering areas where they shouldn't or putting parts of their bodies at risk. For example, a grid can prevent accidental entry into the operating range of a dangerous robot.

As a rule of thumb, any area frequently accessed by unqualified workers or containing moving machinery that could cause injury (such as robots) should be protected with some form of barrier.

## WHOSE RESPONSIBILITY ARE VISUAL AIDS?

In companies with poor Operational Excellence, visual aids are typically installed at the direction of the HSE manager and are limited to HSE matters.

In companies with medium Operational Excellence, area managers also install visual aids to highlight organizational priorities.

In companies with high Operational Excellence, every worker installs visual aids in their own area of responsibility. Workers use these aids for themselves and others: to prevent injuries, emphasize what is important, and improve efficiency and effectiveness.

If you are reading this, feel free to request any visual aids you think are needed in your area from your area manager or HSE manager. Don't wait for them to act; if they haven't been set up so far, they likely won't be set up anytime soon unless you take initiative.

## SUMMARY

**Great companies use visual aids extensively, even when it seems obvious, because they want to make sure it remains obvious even when workers are tired or rushed.**

They make full use of all types of visual aids: posters, poster charts, labels, and barriers.

## ACTION POINTS

1. Are there any tools, bottles, boxes, or shelves that are unlabeled? Label them—or ask the area manager or owner to do so as appropriate.

2. If your subordinates' workplace lacks sufficient posters on Core Values (as defined above), add some.

3. Which poster charts would benefit your subordinates? Create them.

4. Are there any areas under your management that need barriers?

# 9

## PARADIGM SHIFTS

The First Best Practice (**Management Walks**) shifted the paradigm from "a manager's most important work happens in the office" to "a manager's most important work happens in the workplace of their subordinates."

**The Second Best Practice (Audits)** shifted the paradigm from "inspections correct bad behaviors and poor conditions" to "inspections reinforce Core Values and standards."

**The Third Best Practice (Weekly Meetings)** shifted the paradigm from "weekly meetings communicate new information" to "weekly meetings communicate old information (Core Values and standards)."

**The Fourth Best Practice (One-on-one Meetings)** shifted the paradigm from "information flows from managers to employees" to "information flows from employees to managers."

**The Fifth Best Practice (Bright Spot Analysis)** shifted the paradigm from "innovation is about new ideas" to "innovation is about applying proven practices."

**The Sixth Best Practice (Standard Operating Procedures)** shifted the paradigm from "SOPs are about compliance and standardization" to "SOPs are about managing change (hires, promotions, purchases, innovation, etc.)."

**The Seventh Best Practice (Surfacing Problems)** shifted the paradigm from "problem-solving addresses past problems" to "problem-solving prevents future problems."

**The Eighth Best Practice (Visual Aids)** shifted the paradigm from "visual aids ensure compliance under perfect conditions" to "visual aids help avoid mistakes under imperfect conditions (e.g., when employees are rushed or tired)."

**10**

———

# WHAT TO DO NOW

I n the third part of this book, you will find a Roadmap for changing your organization's operational culture. You may, however, want to start small, focusing initially on your direct reports.

The following points will help you prioritize what to do over the next few days.

**TODAY:**

- **Practice the Four Principles in every interaction with your subordinates:** be unmistakably clear, assign unambiguous and rewardable individual objectives, derisk delegation, take visible costly actions, and consistently hold them accountable.

- **Schedule a one-on-one meeting with each subordinate over the next few days.** Book a one-hour slot for each. During the meeting, clarify their individual objectives, including Core Values. Use a blank sheet of paper to write down agreed objectives and how you will evaluate progress. At the end of each meeting, schedule the next one for the following week.

- **Schedule a 30-minute slot for your Management Walks,** following the action items at the end of the "Management Walks" chapter.

- **Schedule two 60-minute slots one week and a month from now** to take the actions listed under the paragraphs titled "One Week from now" and "One Month from Now," found below.

## ONE WEEK FROM NOW:

- **After completing the first round of One-on-one Meetings,** review the sheets where you recorded your subordinates' individual objectives. Note any necessary follow-up actions in your calendar or agenda.

- **In the second and all subsequent rounds of One-on-one Meetings,** review progress against each subordinate's objectives and hold them accountable as agreed. If any issues arise due to past lack of clarity, take responsibility and provide the necessary clarification.

- **Conduct a post-mortem on what you've accomplished so far,** and a pre-mortem on what you plan to do next.

## ONE MONTH FROM NOW:

- **Review the second part of this book, "Best Practices,"** and check whether your actions over the past months align with them. Make any necessary adjustments.

- **Conduct a post-mortem on what you've done so far** and a pre-mortem on what you plan to do next.

**ONWARDS:**

- **Continue implementing the Eight Best Practices of Operational Culture,** and, where appropriate, encourage your subordinates to do the same.

- **Never compromise on Core Values**, no exceptions.

- **Act in accordance with your words.** If you fail to do so, take responsibility and act immediately to ensure it won't happen again for the same reason.

- **Set weekly or monthly 15-minute slots for "Operational Culture Reviews"** to reflect on whether you lived the culture you aim to build and what you need to do differently next week.

- **Schedule half-yearly 2-hour slots** to review this book.

- **Regularly conduct post-mortems** on what you've accomplished **and pre-mortems** on what you plan to do next.

---

*Note: The list above is not comprehensive. Its sole purpose is to provide quick tips on what to start working on as you internalize the concepts covered so far.*

*The third part of this book will offer more guidance on rolling out a change initiative in your organization.*

# PART III

———

# THE ROADMAP TO CHANGE

In the first part of this book, you learned the Four Principles of Operational Excellence:

1. Good managers set unambiguous, individual, and rewardable objectives.

2. Good managers always derisk during delegation and set their subordinates up for success.

3. Good managers demonstrate priorities with visible, costly actions.

4. Good managers are obsessively consistent in holding their subordinates accountable.

In the second part of this book, you learned the Eight Best Practices that transform the Four Principles into visible action:

1. Management Walks

2. Audits

3. Weekly Meetings

4. One-on-one Meetings

5. Bright Spot Analysis

6. Standard Operating Procedures

7. Surfacing Problems

8. Visual Aids

The third part of this book focuses on implementation. It will guide you through planning a change initiative for your team, plant, or company, securing Top Management buy-in, rolling it out, and sustaining it over time.

**1**

———

# GETTING BUY-IN

If you are a member of Top Management, you are likely already familiar with this chapter and can skip to the next one. The following paragraphs are intended for those less experienced in securing buy-in for initiatives that aim to change the operational culture of their team, plant, or company.

## THE NEED FOR PAST EVIDENCE

You should not ask Top Management for support immediately if you lack past evidence of your initiative's effectiveness. Such evidence can take three forms:

- **A successful pilot:** You have already implemented the initiative successfully on a smaller scale in your current company (for example, on a single production line).

- **Previous experience:** You have successfully implemented a similar initiative in a previous company.

- **External experience:** The initiative is being rolled out by external experts, such as a consulting firm or this author.

Unless you work for a startup, do not bother asking Top Management for support unless you have at least one of these three types of evidence. Instead, focus on gathering that evidence. The easiest way is to start with a pilot by rolling out the initiative within your team.

## PRESENTING EVIDENCE

When requesting support from Top Management, you should not only have evidence of your initiative's effectiveness but also present it in a way that is relevant to them.

Avoid focusing too much on technical details: they are important for you, but not for them. Instead, ensure your letter, presentation, or request addresses the following two points.

1. **Past evidence:** As noted earlier, ensure you have evidence that your project will work and highlight it in your request.

2. **ROI:** Every project is evaluated for its ability to generate a high enough Return on Investment. Note that you must not only demonstrate that your initiative's ROI is positive, but also that it is higher than that of competing uses of the company's resources and focus.

You must answer this question explicitly, ***even if not asked***, because they will calculate it anyway, so it's better to do it for them.

To estimate your initiative's bottom-line impact, consider both the benefits of implementation and the costs of inaction. For example, how much does it cost your company to keep producing components at the current defect rate?

Don't forget to consider hidden costs, which are often much larger than the visible ones. For instance, if your company currently suffers from a high injury rate due to a lack of Operational Excellence, the visible costs include lost production time and the expense of managing employee recovery. Hidden costs, however, can be far higher: hiring or training replacements, lower quality from less experienced staff, higher health and safety insurance premiums, and the impact on morale and turnover, as employees are more likely to quit in unsafe environments, leading to additional hiring and training costs, and so on.

## GETTING COMMITMENT

I know consulting firms that only take on engagements from CEOs (or Managing Directors / Plant Managers) who commit to participating in and promoting the initiative. I follow the same approach in my practice, except in very specific cases.

This is crucial. Unless the CEO is the first to participate and set expectations for all employees, your project will not be treated as a priority. As soon as the CEO focuses on another matter, that matter becomes the new priority, and your project fades into obscurity.

So, do not start your initiative until you have a written commitment of personal support from the highest-ranking person in the location or department affected. This may be inconvenient and delay the start, but it will make the entire process much easier.

## INSIST

As a professional, your role is not only to propose initiatives that benefit your company but also to advocate for their implementation.

If Top Management rejects your proposal, do not see it as the end of your initiative. Instead, view it as a sign that your proposal was not fully prepared. Perhaps you didn't understand their perspective or failed to present your case in a way that resonated. Either way, it is your responsibility to try again.

Develop any necessary skills (presentation, writing, finance), make the connections your initiative requires, seek help if appropriate, and then resubmit your proposal.

**2**

———

# ROLLING OUT

Now, let's look at how to roll out your change initiative. It is key to proceed fast but not too fast, spreading yourself too thin, so that you cannot do things well enough for them to work well.

## ACHIEVING CRITICAL MASS

When rolling out an initiative, the key concern is not how many people adopt the desired behaviors, but how geographically concentrated they are. For example, if 20 people in a 200-employee plant adopt a new habit but are scattered across teams, the change will be short-lived. People will see that those around them are not changing and quickly revert to old habits. By contrast, if those 20 people belong to the same team, they will observe the new behavior in those they interact with most, creating a self-sustaining effect.

**In my experience, the main predictor of an initiative's success is whether it achieves critical mass:** whether, in at least one location (team, production line, plant, office floor, etc.), 80–90% of people exhibit the desired behaviors.

Managers have limited time and bandwidth to properly implement the Eight Best Practices of Operational Excellence. They can only apply them fully in a limited area. Trying to change too many people or teams at once scatters attention. While initial results may seem impressive, they quickly fizzle if critical mass is not reached. Therefore, **good managers shrink the scope of change to one location at a time so that they have the necessary bandwidth to pressure the adoption within a critical mass until the new behavior is self-sustaining.**

The Fourth Principle of Operational Excellence emphasizes obsessive consistency: never let an undesired behavior pass even once. Correcting 90% of undesired behaviors across two teams is less effective than correcting 100% on one team and only moving to the next team once the first has internalized the change. One step forward and none back is faster than two steps forward and two steps back.

Similarly, limit the number of behaviors the initiative targets. Attempting to introduce ten new procedures at once is likely to fail, as managers cannot consistently check and reinforce all ten. It is better to spend a month introducing one procedure, obsessively reinforcing it, and only move to the next once the first has been internalized.

**Being too ambitious, targeting too many people or behaviors so that managers cannot fully apply the Fourth Principle, is the main reason change initiatives fail.**

## CAPILLARITY

Why do arteries divide into capillaries? Because blood cells can only exchange oxygen with nearby muscle cells. The same applies to organizations: change requires closeness.

People won't change unless it is communicated in concrete terms and by someone they trust. This must be someone they interact with daily, someone who understands their job, and someone who can explain what the change will mean in practical, concrete terms.

Therefore, **change can only be driven by those close to the people being changed: their direct managers.** They can craft specific, concrete messages, answer questions individually, and show up often enough to earn trust. Because change requires closeness, it can only be scaled using a capillary structure. The CEO initiates it, but it trickles down without skipping levels, from manager to direct reports, repeatedly, until it reaches line workers. At each level, the message becomes more specific and concrete, ensuring **trust is never sacrificed for scale.**

Driving a change initiative is like driving a car. You can only go as fast as you can safely maintain control. Driving faster won't get you to your destination sooner; it will lead to a crash. A skilled driver goes as fast as possible while staying in control. Be like that driver.

## INVOLVING MANAGERS

The CEO must set the expectations for a change initiative to be maximally effective. Otherwise, it will not be treated as a priority and will fizzle out as soon as a new priority arises.

Setting expectations includes personally sending a company-wide email to inform every employee of the initiative, its importance, the CEO's endorsement, and clear expectations (e.g., "I expect every manager to attend training by the end of February, implement the changes in their team by the end of April, and improve this and that indicator by X% by the end of June").

Ideally, the CEO should also speak about the initiative in company-wide meetings, mention it in every internal meeting with more than five people, participate personally in the first training sessions, and discuss it during monthly management walks. Because the CEO's time is valuable, these costly signals are highly effective.

Every other manager and supervisor should be expected to do the same: send team-wide emails, hold public presentations, state clear expectations for subordinates, discuss the initiative in meetings, and reinforce it during Management Walks.

All managers and supervisors, including the CEO, are expected not to let any non-conforming behavior pass. This should be made clear during the expectation-setting phase. Specifically, attending training should be a personal objective for every employee, and failure to do so within a reasonable timeframe should be disciplined.

> "No [team] has time to do optional things. Therefore, training must be mandatory."
>
> — *BEN HOROWITZ*

## CHAPTER SUMMARY

Do not try to push your change initiative faster than your managers' bandwidth allows. Remember, it's not the fastest driver that crosses the finish line first, but the fastest one among those who didn't lose control along the way.

Use the Four Principles and Eight Best Practices of Operational Excellence to ensure your managers dedicate enough time to drive the initiative and reinforce the related habits.

**3**

---

# SUSTAINING

U nless specific systems are established to sustain a change initiative, its results will fade to zero within a few months.

Erosion is a powerful force. Even in companies with great managers, over time, instances where negative behavior is tolerated will accumulate and undermine the positive behaviors built by the initiative. That's why great companies implement systems to counteract erosion.

## FIGHTING EROSION

Mediocre companies assume that once a goal is met (for example, reducing the injury rate below a threshold), attention can shift elsewhere.

Great companies understand that **Operational Culture naturally degrades over time and requires proactive effort to maintain.** They exhibit two key traits. First, they continually emphasize the Four Principles of Operational Excellence, *even when it seems unnecessary.* They educate managers, organize "refresher training sessions," and make the principles central to performance reviews.

Second, they **set costly objectives tied to Core Values-based goals.** A "costly objective" is one that negatively affects both the individual and the company if unmet. For example, if a manager fails to meet their safety objective, their career advancement may be frozen for the year. While risky for the individual, costly objectives effectively shape behavior.

In contrast, "cheap objectives" offer a reward if achieved but no consequence if missed. These are ineffective, as they may encourage managers to neglect one objective to pursue another, such as focusing on production at the expense of safety.

## REWARDING

Good managers are unafraid of clarity. They understand that while a vague objective may seem easier to set, it will inevitably create bigger problems later.

A love of clarity and the boldness to demand it are strong predictors of Operational Excellence. These are the qualities your organization should reward through promotions, raises, or even simple words of appreciation.

## TRAINING

Mandatory refresher training should be held at least once a year to keep employees focused on Core Values, rules, and procedures.

Each manager should be required to organize annual training for all their subordinates. While they may involve Human Resources or external experts to conduct it, the manager remains accountable for attendance and should spend a few minutes at the start setting expectations: What skills should participants learn? What new goals should they be able to achieve?

## INSTITUTIONALIZING YOUR CULTURE

An organization's Culture is the sum of "how we do things here" and the tradeoffs employees consider worthwhile (i.e., the Core Values).

For a Culture to endure, it must be *institutionalized*.

"How we do things here" cannot rely solely on oral tradition. Procedures must be written, stored in visible locations, and enforced. They must become a requirement, not an option, to remain in the organization.

The same applies to Core Values. They should be documented, prominently displayed, and visibly demonstrated by employees and managers. Posters should hang on walls, meetings should begin with a Core Values review, and costly objectives should be tied to them.

**Only an institutionalized Culture lasts.**

## PEER ACCOUNTABILITY

As organizations progress toward Operational Excellence, they will reach a point where Peer Accountability becomes possible.

To define Peer Accountability, I will use the words of Patrick Lencioni:

> "Members of great teams improve their relationship by holding one another accountable, thus demonstrating that they respect each other and have high expectations for one another's performance. [...] A team that avoids accountability creates resentment amongst team members who have different standards of performance [...] and place an undue burden on the team leader as the sole source of discipline [... whereas] the team leader should be the ultimate arbiter when accountability fails."

Peer accountability requires employees to independently recognize the importance of procedures and Core Values. It should not be introduced or expected by organizations still at the early stages of Operational Excellence, where most employees rely on their managers to understand these priorities.

Only once most employees (at least 70–80%) can do so independently can they become interdependent and hold each other accountable.

This is the Holy Grail of Operational Excellence and, in my experience, a very achievable goal when consistently applying the Principles, Best Practices, and Roadmap outlined in this book.

## HIRING

The better the people your organization hires, the easier they are to manage, the better they handle complexity and act autonomously, and the stronger your Operational Culture will be.

Regardless of your role, there are practical steps you can take to improve the quality of hires in your organization.

- **Write precise and compelling job descriptions:** Ensure the description accurately reflects the Operational Culture you want and the qualities required in new hires. A hiring process rarely hires candidates better than the provided job descriptions.

- **Create good career plans:** Do not rely on HR and ensure your hires have strong career plans, as top candidates will expect them. Career plans should be conditional: e.g., "If you achieve this result, you will grow in this direction."

- **Meet potential hires:** As their prospective manager, you are best positioned to assess whether they will fit your team and to influence their decision to join.

- **Do not lie during job interviews:** Misleading candidates may fill the position temporarily, but within a year or two, they will either quit or disengage once they realize the team isn't a good fit.

- **Meet with HR and your bosses in person:** Ask them to recruit the talent your team needs. A brief in-person conversation can encourage them to recommend candidates they might not have otherwise contacted.

- **Ask your subordinates for referrals:** Clearly communicate the desired traits; this also reinforces what is important to your team.

- **Hire multiple people together when possible:** If you need to hire at least two per year, do so simultaneously. Recruiters tend to choose the safest option when hiring a single person, but hiring multiple increases the likelihood of taking calculated risks for better talent.

- **Screen for Core Values:** Refuse candidates who do not share your Core Values and their non-negotiable nature. "Mad geniuses" may seem appealing, but they often cause more harm than good. This is particularly true if you aren't a team at the leading edge of innovation.

- **Maintain a strong team atmosphere:** Focus on fairness and respect rather than perks or events. A healthy environment encourages subordinates to recommend good hires and speak positively about your team.

- **Ask exit questions proactively:** Do not wait for someone to express a desire to quit to ask: "If you were to leave the company in the next few years, what would be the reason?"

- **Use Bright Spot Analysis (Best Practice #5).** Who in your organization has the best track record at hiring? Learn from them and involve them more in hiring.

## CHAPTER SUMMARY

Never commit the mistake of believing that things are going so well that you can get away with forgetting about the Four Principles and Eight Best Practices. They are the reason things are going so well, and things will get worse if you forget about them.

Aggressively reinforce good behavior even when it seems ingrained. Never let your people wonder whether it still matters.

# CONCLUSIONS

Congratulations on making it this far! You now know the Four Principles of Operational Excellence, the Eight Best Practices to apply them, and a Roadmap for implementing change in your organization.

Never forget that Operational Excellence is, above all, about Clarity. Strive for maximum clarity in all situations, avoiding behaviors or circumstances that create confusion or ambiguity, and you will succeed.

Set up the necessary systems and take the actions required to ensure everyone in the company does the same, and your organization will thrive.

## WHAT TO DO NOW?

Now it's time to put what you've learned in this book into practice in your company.

Have confidence in yourself, the Four Principles, and the Eight Best Practices.

If you apply them consistently and relentlessly, results will follow.

———

The author, Luca Dellanna, has over twelve years of experience consulting corporations worldwide. **If you would like his help with an initiative to improve your organization's Operational Culture, do not hesitate to email him at Luca@Luca-dellanna.com**

For bulk purchases of this book to share with colleagues, special pricing is available. Contact Luca at the same address. He can even conduct an in-person or virtual workshop for you and your team.

Luca also has a newsletter in which he regularly posts new essays: Luca-Dellanna.com/newsletter.

———

All the best for your journey towards Operational Excellence!

# AFTERWORD

If you found this book useful, please recommend it to your friends and colleagues.

It would mean a lot if you could write a review on Amazon or Goodreads—whichever is easier for you. **Your recommendation or review would truly make my day.**

———

I publish about one book a year. If you want to be notified of my new publications, you can subscribe to my newsletter at **Luca-dellanna.-com/newsletter.**

I also regularly write on Twitter. Contrary to many authors who use it only for promotion purposes, I tend to reward my readers' attention rather than consuming it. You can follow me on **twitter.-com/dellannaluca**

If you have any questions, do not hesitate to email me. My address is **Luca@Luca-dellanna.com**

I hold weekly and monthly sessions (face-to-face and over the Internet) with some of my clients, in which I help them advance their careers and personal lives beyond the advice provided in this book. If you would be interested in joining, don't hesitate to email me.

———

To the next book, and good luck changing the Operational Culture of your organization and achieving Operational Excellence!

# ABOUT THE AUTHOR
## LUCA DELLANNA

Luca has been supporting senior leaders on risk-, operations-, and people- management as an independent expert for over 12 years.

For some clients, he acts as an on-demand advisor to provide expertise in his areas of competence. For others, he conducts short workshops to efficiently increase the managerial capabilities of their leaders. Sometimes, he also conducts short on-site consulting engagements and benchmark audits.

In addition to his advisory activity, Luca is an external lecturer at an Italian university and frequently speaks at conferences and internal company events. Luca is also the author of eleven books and an independent researcher in economics, behavioral sciences, and public health, and has presented at large conferences and won international research grants.

Trained as an automotive engineer, Luca led large teams and consulted for large multinationals before quitting his corporate job in 2015 to become an independent advisor, researcher, and author. After living in Spain, Germany, and Singapore, he returned to his home-town of Turin (Italy).

Luca writes regularly on Twitter (**@DellAnnaLuca**). You can visit his website at **Luca-dellanna.com**. You can also contact him at **Luca@luca-dellanna.com** *(he reads all emails personally)*.

In the following pages, you can find a brief overview of Luca's other books. You can support him by recommending this book to your friends or colleagues and leaving a review on Amazon.

X  x.com/DellAnnaLuca

in  linkedin.com/in/dellannaluca

▶  youtube.com/LucaDellannaChannel

# ALSO BY LUCA DELLANNA

Poverty and Prosperity (2026)

Winning Long-Term Games (2024)

Managing Hybrid and Remote Teams, 2$^{nd}$ ed. (2024)

Ergodicity: How Irreversible Outcomes Affect Long-term Performance in Work, Investing, Relationships, Sport, and Beyond, 3$^{rd}$ ed. (2023)

The Employee Engagement Handbook (2023)

The Pandemic Guidebook (2022)

100 Truths You Will Learn Too Late, 3$^{rd}$ ed. (2021)

Teams Are Adaptive Systems (2020)

The Control Heuristic, 2$^{nd}$ ed. (2020)

The Power of Adaptation (2018)

The World Through a Magnifying Glass, 2$^{nd}$ ed. (2018)

**ERGODICITY**

How Irreversible Outcomes Affect Long-term Performance in Work, Investing, Relationships, Sport, and Beyond (3rd ed.)

"This is one of the most important books I've read, period. It's short, articulate, and expansive on a singular subject matter — ergodicity, which is really the key ingredient to success in life, marriage, business, family, happiness, health, etc."

*— BLAKE JANOVER, JANOVER INC. CEO*

"A great book for those who quickly want to familiarize themselves with the concept of ergodicity. The author goes to great lengths to explain the concept in easily understandable terms. Highly recommended!"

*—AUKE HUNNEMAN*

# THE CONTROL HEURISTIC: THE NATURE OF HUMAN BEHAVIOR (2<sup>ND</sup> ED.)

"This book is like a magnificent suspension bridge, linking the science of the human brain to the practical craft of applying it in everyday life. I loved it."

*— RORY SUTHERLAND*

"A SUPERB book [...] by one of the profound thinkers in our field [behavioral economics]."

*— MICHAL G. BARTLETT*

"Luca's book was so helpful to my work. Opened my eyes up to some more reasons why change is so hard."

*— CHRIS MURMAN*

"Lots of specific and practical advice! Even experienced managers should find each chapter hugely valuable for reassessing their performance in each of the areas.

— *GABY LLOYD*

"Packed full of useful information. Luca takes the maddeningly difficult subject of managing a team and breaks it down into actionable activities. The sections on Clarity and Feedback are particularly strong, providing a way of viewing management as a nurturing and human activity.

— *DANIEL WEBB*

"Thought-provoking."

— *CARL BROWN*

## WINNING LONG-TERM GAMES

The key to winning long-term games is to stop playing them as a succession of *separate* short-term games.

Yet, most people take the opposite approach. Here are three examples:

- The manager who sees each interaction with her team as a *separate* game. Every time she talks to her subordinates, it's to get things done rather than develop their skills. As a result, she fails to build the long-term assets (a competent team) she needs in order to win her long-term game (a successful career).

- The spouse who lies to avoid responsibility. If lying has, say, a 1% chance of being discovered, it is a great short-term tactic (it succeeds 99% of the time) but a terrible long-term strategy (if you lie once a week, you have a 99.5% chance of getting caught over a decade).

- The solopreneur who sends weekly emails to their mailing list and sees each as a *separate* game. They *consume* their audience's trust to generate more sales within a single email instead of *building* trust to create more sales within a few months.

These three examples show that approaching long-term games as a succession of *separate* short-term games is a bad strategy *despite working great over short time horizons.*

In "Winning Long-Term Games," Luca guides the reader into designing strategies that not only have a long-term horizon but also *leverage the long term* to gain an edge against anyone with shorter time horizons and make success all but inevitable.

*Winning Long-Term Games is planned to be published in the first half of 2024.*

"I am amazed at Luca Dellanna's ability to observe, compile, and articulate 99 very actionable life principles here. Each chapter describes the rule in a way that makes you think and then summarizes the Action. It's filled with DEEP insights yet VERY readable."

— *THERESIA TANZIL*

"Absolutely brilliant. You might have grasped some of these concepts before, but having them structured and in writing makes all the difference [...] I will surely recommend it to friends and co-workers."

— *ALBERTO PISANELLO*

"A very thoughtful piece of writing, deep and wiring!"

— *DAVID KREJCA*

# THE WORLD THROUGH A MAGNIFYING GLASS (2<sup>ND</sup> ED.)

"Thank you for helping me understand! My son was recently diagnosed, and I needed to be able to understand how he views the world. Why would certain things overwhelm him and cause so much anxiety and pain. This book made it so clear and easy to understand."

*— GEIGER T.*


Probably one of the best works I have read on autism (I have read a few), and it's surprising how realistically he depicts the condition."

*— MANEL VILAR*


"Loved The World Through a Magnifying Glass – this analogy NAILS IT."

*— EMERSON SPARTZ, NYT BESTSELLER AUTHOR*

# ACKNOWLEDGMENTS

To Wenlin Tan, for providing me with love and support.

To my mother for supporting and loving me all my life, and to Franco for loving her.

To my father, for the same and for stirring intellectual curiosity within me.

To my former colleagues during my years in Frankfurt, and especially to my bosses, Christian, Andreas, Michele, and Marcelino, who had confidence in me and introduced me to the world of Management Consulting and Operational Excellence in an ethical and long-term way.

To my friends and everyone else who, directly or indirectly, knowingly or unknowingly, contributed to my well-being.

To my Patrons Ross Screaton, Malcolm Ocean, Ricardo Ortiz Noguera, and Pablo Cárdenas. Their help gave me stability on top of which I could conduct my research.

To Ritvars Eglājs, for having surfaced a typo in a previous edition.

To everyone I quoted in this book and to everyone I follow on Twitter, their inspiration was fundamental. I wrote this book on the shoulders of giants.

# FURTHER READINGS



"**Managing Hybrid and Remote Teams,**" by Luca Dellanna (myself), on how to manage teams for effectiveness and engagement.

**The Control Heuristic**" by Luca Dellanna (myself), on why changing habits is so hard.

"**High Output Management,**" by former Intel CEO Andy Grove, on managing teams.

"**Scaling People,**" by Claire Hughes Johnson, on how to build corporate HR systems. Make sure you download the additional materials PDF mentioned in the book: half of the value of the book is in there.

"**An Elegant Puzzle: Systems of Engineering Management,**" by Will Larson. Highly recommended for corporate directors, less so for smaller companies or less senior roles.

"**The Hard Thing About Hard Things**" and "**What You Do Is Who You Are**" by Silicon Valley entrepreneur Ben Horowitz.

"**The Four Obsessions of an Extraordinary Executive**" by Patrick Lencioni, though his other books on leadership are excellent, too.

"**Alchemy,**" by Ogilvy's vice-chairman Rory Sutherland, on the importance of the non-legible.

"**It Doesn't Have To Be Crazy at Work,**" by Basecamp founders Jason Fried and David Heinemeier Hansson, for how an excellent workplace doesn't have to squeeze every bit of energy from its employees.

"**Skin In The Game,**" by Nassim Nicholas Taleb, for why accountability has to be fully assigned.

PART IV

---

# APPENDIX

This section contains parts that were present in the first edition of this book but were removed from the core to keep it more concise.

Let's explore three problems most managers like you face: managing difficult employees, getting the time to do everything, and creating an environment of trust.

Of course, this is not an exhaustive list—there are more urgent and more important problems—but these are some of the most common ones.

**1**

---

# MANAGING DIFFICULT EMPLOYEES

By "difficult employees," I mean those who chronically lack motivation, resist changes, react adversarially to training, or lack the discipline to work in a team. These seemingly different groups share the same root cause: they do not know that good individual outcomes follow achieving objectives, or have forgotten it, or have been taught otherwise by bad managers, or believe it does not apply in their company.

Some never learned this link because they lacked the skills or were never rewarded by teachers and managers. Others spent months or years under managers who failed to set attainable objectives, provide support, or reward achievement, causing them to forget the connection.

In some cases, the issue is not learning that bad behavior leads to bad outcomes. This happens when, at work or school, the employee behaves badly, faces no punishment, and benefits instead—for example, arriving late to meetings without consequence, learning that bad behavior goes unpunished.

In rare cases, other reasons may underlie underperformance or bad behavior, but the reasons above explain the vast majority. Difficult employees act this way because they have lived in a paradigm where bad behavior is more advantageous than productive behavior.

The solution is simple, though hard: **managers must let them experience a different paradigm where bad behavior consistently leads to negative outcomes and good behavior to positive ones.** The keyword is consistently. Most managers reward achievement, but often less consistently than they let it go unrewarded. People remember the one time their efforts went to waste more than the nine times they were rewarded. Unless managers are obsessively consistent in enforcing promised consequences, their words lose force. **Inconsistency debases authority;** respect, trust, and authority are earned through consistency, and a single lapse can ruin months of effort and create motivational losses.

Many managers feel they lack the time and resources to reward employees consistently. The next chapter, *Getting the Time to Do Everything,* addresses this issue.

Similarly, **when facing an indifferent subordinate, managers should teach him again that good outcomes follow good performance and that such performance is attainable.** Managers do not need to teach a demotivated subordinate to produce results; they need to teach him that producing results brings good individual outcomes. These are two different concepts, and focusing on the former when the bottleneck is the latter sets managers up for frustration. (Of course, if lack of skills—not motivation—limits performance, managers must ensure the necessary know-how is provided.)

## CATCH THEM RIGHT

**Teach subordinates the correct paradigm by creating opportunities to learn that fulfilling objectives brings good outcomes.** Start with small objectives and reward their achievement mainly with words of appreciation (other rewards should be reserved for excellent performers).

Managers should reward only efforts that achieve objectives. They should not praise unachieved efforts but may acknowledge them and stress that results matter, while also providing a clear path toward those results. If the employee fails, whether by trying and failing or failing to try, assign a smaller objective. Never endlessly lower objectives, hoping to catch him succeeding without consequence.

An important exception: **the employee must not learn that doing less means being asked less. Always make clear that performance so far has been subpar and that minimum standards apply, including possible dismissal** where the law allows. If lowering the bar is impossible, increase the time spent focusing on the employee. When he succeeds, do not immediately raise the bar; instead, first reinforce good behavior for at least one or two weeks.

**This process may seem utopian, but it works. When it fails, it is usually because it was not implemented consistently or clearly.** An employee's performance is capped by the lesser of their skill, their internal drive, and the consistency with which they've been taught to expect good outcomes for good performance and bad outcomes for bad performance. (The Fourth Principle of Operational Excellence covered this in depth.)

Rewards should match the size of the objective. Excessive rewards, especially compared to those given to stronger performers, teach sloppiness. For small objectives, use sincere praise such as "Good job." If the result helped the team, add why: "Good job, this was helpful because..."

If you fairly reward a "difficult employee" for achieving an objective, he will begin to link fulfilling objectives with good outcomes. Sometimes one success starts a virtuous circle; sometimes it takes many. Always reward results, not effort. Otherwise, you'll have a team signaling effort instead of delivering results. Effort not contributing to organizational success should not be praised, though it is respectful to acknowledge it: "I noticed the effort, but you did not achieve the objective, and that is what matters." Objectives must also be human and sustainable (remember the First Principle of Operational Excellence?).

Sometimes it helps to "carve a role" for difficult employees. Like Dennis Rodman in basketball, famous for excelling at rebounding, find a skill or interest they have that others lack, but that is relevant to your business. Assign small objectives around it to build pride in their work ethic. Work ethic is contagious and can spread to other areas.

**Do not only ask what a person can do for their job; ask what they can do for the organization.** Some employees are weak in the former but valuable in the latter. Allocating part of their time to the latter can boost their confidence, engagement, and eventually their main performance.

To summarize,

1. Give the difficult employee objectives he can achieve.

2. Catch them doing something right.

3. If they do, thank or praise appropriately, then raise the bar gradually.

4. If they do not, lower the bar and try again.

Operational Excellence means clarifying the link between achieving objectives and individual outcomes.

## MOTIVATIONAL LOSSES

**Every time an employee believes they did a good job but are not rewarded appropriately, they suffer a motivational loss.** Some employees are more internally driven and can endure a few such losses without visible impact, but everyone has a "breaking point." After enough motivational losses, even the most engaged employee may lose enthusiasm, become difficult, or leave the company.

Managers must therefore avoid motivational losses in their subordinates, starting with clear objectives. If an objective is ambiguous, a subordinate may genuinely believe they met it and then be told their work was insufficient, experiencing a major motivational loss as expected praise turns into reprimand.

Unambiguous objectives are essential to prevent motivational losses.

## TOXIC EMPLOYEES

Notwithstanding the above, some employees are not merely "difficult" but also "toxic." While difficult employees have forgotten (or never learned) the link between fulfilling objectives and good outcomes, toxic employees operate from beliefs and paradigms that damage the team's Operational Culture.

Difficult employees should be treated as potential assets and trained accordingly; toxic ones as liabilities. If local legislation permits, steps should be taken to let them go. In my experience, companies often both overestimate the share of toxic employees (most are simply difficult) and underestimate the urgency of removing the truly toxic ones.

Firing toxic employees may seem cruel, but keeping them is crueler, to colleagues (whose efforts are devalued), to the company (which bears the burden), and even to the employee (who may benefit from a new environment or a clear signal that change is required for good outcomes). Firing should remain a last resort, used only after sincerely giving the employee chances and support to change, to confirm that their toxicity is inherent rather than a temporary reaction to an unconducive environment.

## SUMMARY

If you have difficult employees, you need to get them to experience the link between fulfilling objectives and good personal outcomes.

1. Give them achievable objectives.

2. Catch them doing something right, such as fulfilling objectives or following rules.

3. If they do so, thank or praise them appropriately, then raise the bar, but not too much.

4. If they do not, lower the bar and try again, while making it clear your tolerance won't be infinite.

**2**

———

# GETTING THE TIME TO DO EVERYTHING

As a manager, you will often face days with too much to do and too little time. Many respond by working longer hours. This may be necessary during exceptional deadlines, such as year-end, but doing it too often is unwise. Chronic overtime brings stress and jadedness, increasing mistakes and limiting professional growth.

**In companies with poor Operational Excellence, overtime may signal commitment; in companies with good Operational Excellence, it signals structural problems such as poor prioritization and inefficiency.** I once overheard an executive saying he could not promote an employee who regularly worked long hours: promotion would overload them further, forcing either burnout or underperformance. Imagine the employee's shock: they thought overtime would boost his career!

Being understaffed may temporarily explain a high workload, but not in the long term. A competent organization reacts quickly to unexpected staff loss or business growth by hiring. Failure to do so usually means one of three things: top management lacks competence or commitment, the business is weak (shrinking or unprofitable), or managers are poor at prioritizing. If the first two apply, consider changing companies to avoid an uphill battle. If the third applies (poor prioritization), the rest of this chapter will help you.

## THE SOURCE OF PROBLEMS

Each problem has a root cause. For example, subordinates may keep asking you questions on the same topic because they lack clarity or know-how. If you answer without training them to find answers themselves, they will keep returning with the same questions, consuming your time.

Root causes continually generate problems. Solving only the visible issues while ignoring the root cause means the problems will keep coming, like bailing water from a sinking ship without fixing the hole.

**Almost anyone with a time problem actually has a prioritization problem. They work on superficial, urgent issues while waiting for a "perfect day" to address root causes.** That day never arrives. Problems end only when you decide to tackle their root causes despite the pressures you face.

## MANAGING THE URGENT

Every day brings something urgent, making it hard to find time for what's truly important: addressing root causes. **The very important rarely looks urgent.** Solving root causes will always seem less pressing than solving the problems they create.

**Good managers are not fooled by urgency. They work on the important even when it doesn't appear urgent, ignoring the urgent if necessary. They understand that unless they do so, they will never have time to work on the truly important.**

Companies with poor Operational Culture reward managers who tackle the urgent; those with good culture reward managers who tackle the important.

This does not mean the urgent cannot be important; it means priorities should be set solely by importance, regardless of urgency.

## GETTING MORE TIME

It may seem that each subordinate is a constant source of problems. If you only solve the problems they bring you, they will keep bringing more, limited only by your availability. **Spend time today training them to solve problems themselves, and tomorrow you will have far more time because they will no longer depend on you.**

**Of course, you cannot train all subordinates on all issues at once. But today, you can train one subordinate on one recurring problem.** Tomorrow you will save time because that problem will no longer reach you. Use that saved time to train another subordinate on another issue. Repeating this day after day, within months, you'll free up much more time.

If subordinates repeatedly bring you questions on the same topic that require context-based answers, appoint a subject matter expert (a senior employee responsible for handling those questions), freeing you to do your job.

Remember that **delegating tasks outside your job description is not laziness. It is lazy to do them yourself to avoid the emotional work of focusing on what is truly critical for your role.**

The same applies to problems from customers, bosses, peers, bureaucracy, and so on. Every recurring problem has a root cause that generates new instances. Work on it rather than the symptoms; that is the only way to stop facing the same problems over and over.

**Chronic problems are life's way of telling you to directly address a source of problems you haven't addressed yet,** at least not directly.

## A GOOD QUESTION

If you continue spending your workdays as you have been recently, what will your team's Operational Culture look like in a few years?

What will your own work life look like?

## ACTION POINT

Make a list of recurring problems that consume your time, and identify the one that takes the most. Can you take any action today to reduce future time wasted on it? Can you address its root cause?

**3**

---

# CREATING TRUST

As a manager, you want your subordinates' trust. Trust leads them to share information, escalate problems early (so that you can catch them before they're too large), and work faster and more effectively on assigned objectives. However, trust must be earned. Here are the key requirements and how to achieve them:

**1. Competence: Subordinates will not trust your decisions if they doubt your competence.** Perceived competence depends on two factors: your track record (past results and team performance) and whether you listen to subordinates and explain your decisions. Subordinates may disagree with your decisions, but if they believe you truly know their problems and perspective, they are less likely to resent you. Conversely, if they feel unheard, disagreement will be seen as incompetence, damaging trust.

**2. Visibility: Subordinates must see you spend time at their workplace for them to believe you truly know their jobs and their challenges.** Meeting them only in your office or conference rooms creates the impression that you are disconnected. Hence, the importance of the first and second Best Practices (Management Walks and Mini Audits).

**3. Fairness: Enforce rules and evaluate people fairly, predictably, and consistently.** No favorites, exceptions, or judgments based on effort or circumstances. Double standards or subjective judgments make decisions appear personal, reducing trust.

**4. Principled behavior.** Counterintuitively, people cannot fully trust someone loyal to individuals. What if they have to decide between two people they swore loyalty to? Only people who are loyal to principles can be fully trusted, for their behavior won't depend on circumstances.

## DO NOT DEBASE YOUR AUTHORITY

Bad managers think their authority comes from their titles. In reality, relying on job titles for coercion produces only minimal performance, and only while they are watching.

Conversely, **good managers know authority comes from consistency in keeping their word**, especially regarding the consequences of achieving or failing to achieve objectives. **A respected manager is one whose objectives lead to positive outcomes when completed and negative consequences when not.**

Here are some behaviors that debase authority:

- Failing to acknowledge those who meet objectives.

- Setting objectives that, if completed, add no value (e.g., preparing a report no one will read).

- Asking for actions that, if neglected, carry no negative consequences (e.g., safety rules that are ignored without consequence).

And here are some behaviors that build authority:

- Setting objectives and following up with proportional rewards or reprimands.

- Setting objectives that produce tangible improvements for the team or organization.

- Always following through on commitments ("You didn't send the report I requested yesterday. That's a problem because I need it for tomorrow's decision. When I ask, it's important.").

- Judging fairly, reinforcing authority for both the manager and the principles applied.

Authority is the track record that one's word can be taken seriously and that doing so will lead to good outcomes.

# HIGHLIGHTS

**FROM THE FIRST PRINCIPLE OF OPERATIONAL EXCELLENCE**

When managers fail to execute on performance management, they compromise the good results they might have obtained in other areas.

The more ambiguous an objective, the higher the chances that a worker misinterprets it and fails to fulfill it. Lack of clarity makes it challenging for managers to hold their subordinates accountable.

Managers who set ambiguous objectives tend to have underperforming subordinates and are less likely to hold them accountable for their underperformance.

Once a manager has let someone off the hook, they set a precedent for others, making it easier for them to argue that they should also be given a pass. This makes it even more difficult for the manager to be consistent in applying consequences in the future and further deteriorates the team's operational culture.

Managers who set unclear and unambitious objectives cannot reward those employees who performed and cannot punish those who didn't. Consequently, the team underperforms.

Good managers are aware of the vicious circle of bad performance management. They prevent it by setting clear objectives and by being fully consistent in applying consequences.

**When managers fail to set clear objectives, it is not because of a lack of skills. Rather, it is because of some mental patterns that make them believe that setting *unclear* objectives is the optimal choice.**

**Guilt and shame by a manager are symptoms of insufficient clarity, individuality, or ambition during delegation.**

Good managers do not wait for the perfect environment to do their work; rather, they realize that it's *their* job to create a conducive environment.

When good managers spot a lack of motivation in their subordinates, they interpret it as a signal of a lack of clarity of objectives, personal impact, or individual outcomes.

Setting clear and ambitious objectives and guaranteeing fair consequences is helpful and generous. Conversely, managers who are ambiguous in their objectives' definitions and inconsistent in their application are selfish. To feel more comfortable with themselves, they limit their subordinates' potential.

Chronically requiring overtime is a sign of a dysfunctional company that tries to compensate for its structural problems by burdening its employees.

Chronically doing overtime is a sign of a dysfunctional manager who tries to cover his effectiveness problem by throwing more time and energy into problems that do not need it.

Indifference and laziness are symptoms of having forgotten that good outcomes follow good performance.

The manager has to create the conditions to be able to "catch the subordinate doing something good."

Bad managers try to achieve alignment through communication; good managers achieve alignment by rewarding behaviors that align with the organization's objectives.

Whenever managers make the "easy choice" and sacrifice clarity, fairness, or consistency to avoid a difficult conversation or a difficult choice, they incur "management debt": a subjective short-term gain that will eventually have to be paid back with interest.

**The more managers make "easy choices" by sacrificing clarity, fairness, or consistency, the more their subordinates will make "easy choices" themselves by sacrificing performance, quality, and teamwork.**

## FROM THE SECOND PRINCIPLE OF OPERATIONAL EXCELLENCE

The opposite of micromanagement isn't good management but a lack of management.

Vague objectives don't create freedom but paralysis.

Being specific on what matters is good: be clear about what success looks like, what resources the delegee can use, what boundaries they must respect, and any procedures critical for success.

Great managers know that every extra minute spent setting delegees up for success saves at least two minutes of problem-solving later.

You must be superclear: not just clear enough so that you can be understood, but clear enough so that you cannot be misunderstood.

To keep your team engaged, they should succeed at least 70% of the time and receive praise for it.

Never delegate non-trivial tasks over email.

If your delegees do not satisfactorily complete about 70–80% of your assigned tasks, or if you spend more time fixing their mistakes than delegating, it means you are not investing enough time upfront to set them up for success.

A subordinate who isn't successful will not only underperform but also quickly lose motivation and trust in you.

Do not let the fear of being seen as a micromanager stop you from doing your job: setting your people up for success.

## FROM THE THIRD PRINCIPLE OF OPERATIONAL EXCELLENCE

The reason why Core Values are so difficult to adopt in the day-to-day Operations is that they represent short-term costs.

Good managers know that one reason employees do not practice Core Values is that they are fearful of potential punishments for not being productive in the short term. Therefore, they personally take visible actions, incurring these costs, to show that they are truly worth paying.

Good managers use both words and actions. The costlier the action, the stronger its effect on getting Core Values internalized.

Culture is not made of perks and terminology but of time-consuming and cost-intensive rituals that are conspicuously perceived as worth it.

## FROM THE FOURTH PRINCIPLE OF OPERATIONAL EXCELLENCE

**Bad managers are volatile in how they apply the standards they set. They believe that workers respond to the average application of the standard, but instead, workers remember the extremes.**

Consistent judgment on unambiguous objectives whose specifics have been clear since the beginning cannot be unfair.

**If managers reward effort, eventually, their subordinates will spend their time showing effort rather than getting results.**

Good managers set targets high enough that their completion brings enough windfall to be redistributed across their team.

Good managers understand that failing to notice that the work was subpar will, counterintuitively, lead to their best team members getting demotivated.

Good managers are fair and loyal to principles, not loyal to people.

## FROM THE REST OF THE BOOK

It's not that most managers do not reward achieving objectives. They do. However, often, they do it less consistently than they let having achieved objectives go unrewarded. Unfortunately, people are more likely to remember that one time when their efforts went to waste rather than those nine times when they got rewarded.

**Your main tasks as a manager are making the important unmistakable and conspicuous and consistently rewarding people based on their results against their personal objectives and on stewarding Core Values.**

Do not assume that your subordinates already know how their efforts contribute to others, and do not assume that telling them is an insult to their intelligence. People need to be explicitly reminded of the worth of their efforts, even if they are already aware of it.

As a manager, it is both your job to help your subordinates understand the meaning of their work and to ensure that they are, in turn, helping their own subordinates do the same.

**Decisions made in the manager's office remain there. Managers do not have the power to affect the way of working of their subordinates unless they translate them into visible actions at their subordinates' workplaces.**

Either the rule or procedure has to be rewritten, or the worker has to acknowledge that he shouldn't have acted that way. There is no grey area in between, no one-off exception. Letting an exception pass once is how exceptions become the new norm. Good managers never allow that.

It is everyone's responsibility to hold peers, subordinates, and superiors accountable for rules, standards, and Core Values.

When calling out something wrong, managers should always direct the feedback or the critique towards the behavior of an employee, never to the employee personally.

**When asking questions, give your subordinates the authority to answer them.**

**The main function of Weekly Meetings is to reinforce the Core Values and Operational Culture of the organization.**

People need to be repeatedly reminded of the importance of whatever is not the default state, for they progressively revert to it otherwise.

**Good managers know that, no matter how many times Core Values have been mentioned during Weekly Meetings, if during a single**

**Weekly Meeting they are not mentioned, doubt regarding their importance and uncompromisability will rise again among its attendees.**

Weekly meetings are exceptional communication tools because the manager has the opportunity to talk to their whole team at the same time. Each attendee will know that whatever expectation has been set during the meeting, each other attendee heard it as well.

Conspicuousness – setting expectations in a way that is visible to everyone – is a great way to influence the actions of others effectively.

Good managers not only communicate to get every subordinate to know and embrace what has to be done; they also communicate to make sure that every subordinate knows that everyone else in the team knows and embraces what has to be done. Weekly meetings are a great channel to do that.

If a comment is made about someone's personality, the manager should immediately refocus it on that person's behavior.

Before the meeting ends, the manager has to ensure that every participant walks out the door committed to doing whatever task was assigned to them during the meeting, even if they did not agree on it.

Ideally, meetings should follow the "disagree and commit" model.

Passive commitment is equal to passive sabotage.

**Great managers demand conflict (by asking everyone to voice their concerns), then demand commitment (by asking everyone to promise what they will do), and finally demand results (by letting everyone know that they will be held accountable for doing whatever the team decides).**

One-on-one Meetings should last at least half an hour, even if there is nothing to discuss, especially if there is nothing to discuss. This is because there is always something to discuss.

Buffers prevent problems from surfacing until it's too late. Just In Time (and other techniques that reduce buffers) allow problems to surface so that they can be solved before it's too late.

**Problems grow to the size they need in order to be acknowledged. An organization that is slow in acknowledging problems will find itself with big problems.**

Measuring trends at the bottom of the pyramid allows us to be proactive and prevent negative events, whereas measuring trends at the top causes us to be reactive and suffer from negative events.

By tying consequences (rewards and punishments) to leading indicators in addition to lagging ones, the frequency of negative events increases, causing the incentive to optimize for the frequent small profits to disappear.

If a bad performance on a lagging indicator does not impact the employee in any way, then he will not change his behavior.

Shortcuts are the shortest way to another instance of the same problem.

Incident investigations are as effective as the level of the highest person involved.

Some managers dismiss the importance of posters by saying that their subordinates already know what's written on them. These managers forget that **Communication doesn't happen when a message is first said; it happens when it can no longer be mistaken.**

Labels (and visual aids in general) are not there to protect against inexperience. They are there to protect against fatigue, rushing, and other mental conditions that might cause an otherwise competent operator to commit a mistake.

**Great companies do not only use visual aids for difficult-to-remember items; they also use them for important-to-remember items, regardless of whether they're obvious.**

In my experience, the main predictor of whether an initiative will succeed is whether it achieves critical mass: whether, in at least one location (a team, a production line, a plant, an office floor, etc.), 80-90% of the people are exhibiting the desired behaviors.

"No [team] has time for optional things. Therefore, training must be mandatory."—*Ben Horowitz.*

The more an employee is toward the right of the Adoption Curve spectrum, the higher the percentage of his colleagues who need to adopt the procedure for him to be willing to do so. Therefore, managers of large divisions who focus their efforts on all subordinates at the same time in the same way are bound to fail. Instead, change initiatives must be progressively rolled out. First, to innovators. Then, to the early majority. Only afterward, to the rest of the team. The adoption of the former two groups is needed to recruit the latter one.

**Great companies exhibit the following two traits. First, they keep talking about the Four Principles of Operational Excellence, even when they do not seem necessary anymore. Second, they keep placing costly objectives on the achievement of Core Values-based goals.**

Instead of conducting exit interviews, ask people who left your team why they did so. Ask them these questions while they are still your team members.

**Only institutionalized Culture lasts.**

# NOTES

## Introduction

1. Source: *"Two Centuries of Process Safety at DuPont"*, James A. Klein, 2009, Wiley Inter-Science, DOI 10.1002/prs.10309

2. I did not and do not endorse DuPont's stance or actions on many matters, including OGMs, which I strongly criticize. At the time, I was ignorant of the topic and did not know about its risks. I only worked there for the consulting division, which helped other companies work better and safer.

## 2. The 2nd Principle of Operational Excellence

1. Under-delivery is undesirable both because of its high opportunity cost (the delegee could have saved some time and used it to work on something else) and because it leads to motivational losses (the delegee expected to be praised for the over-delivery, but the manager cannot praise them if that was a poor use of their time).

# CONTENTS

www.ingramcontent.com/pod-product-compliance
Lightning Source LLC
Chambersburg PA
CBHW040140160726
48006CB00014B/1559